INSIDE L.A. ART

INSIDE L.A. ART

A Guide to Museums and Galleries
from Santa Barbara to San Diego

DEBORAH ASHIN

CHRONICLE BOOKS/SAN FRANCISCO

To my husband, Daniel

Copyright ©1980 by Deborah Ashin
All rights reserved
Printed in the United States of America.

Library of Congress Cataloging in Publication Data
Ashin, Deborah
   Inside L.A. Art

Includes index.
   1.   Art museums—California—Los Angeles metropolitan
area—Guide-books.   I.   Title.
N511.C2A84   708.194'9   80-22527
ISBN 0-87701-153-2

Editing and design by Harper & Vandenburgh
Composition by HMS Typographers
Cover photo by Robert Landau
Cover design by Howard Jacobsen

Photo Credits:
Frank J. Thomas: p. 6; Don Hull: p. 9;
courtesy of The Gamble House: p. 40;
courtesy of Forest Lawn Museum: p. 48;
courtesy of Los Angeles Municipal Arts
Department: p. 57; courtesy of ARCO
Center for Visual Art: p. 59; courtesy of
California State University, Long Beach:
p. 72; courtesy of Harry A. Franklin Gallery: p. 84.

Chronicle Books
870 Market Street
San Francisco, CA 94102

ACKNOWLEDGMENTS

I would like to express my gratitude to the many people who have made this book a reality: to Daniel G. Sadler for his invaluable guidance, rewriting, and encouragement; to Patrice Badstubner for her moral and editorial support; to Beth Kelly for her blitz at the typewriter; to all of the museums and galleries for their assistance and cooperation; to the Southern California RTD for identifying the correct bus routes; and to my parents, Judith and Jay Ashin. And finally, to the artists whose vision and creativity link us with history and give texture to our lives, and without whom there would be no galleries and no art museums.

TABLE OF CONTENTS

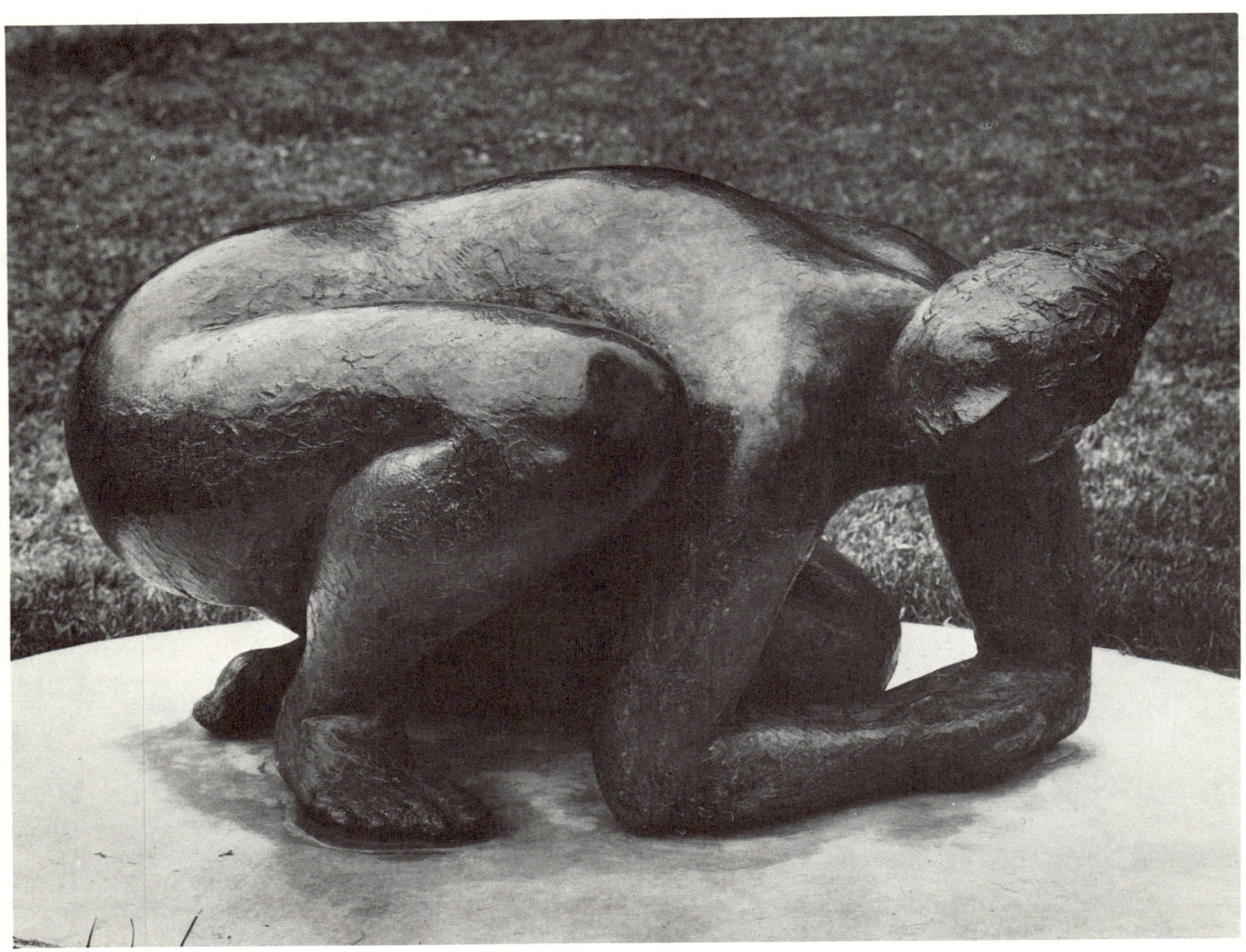

Desnudo Reclinado, Francisco Zuñiga
Franklin D. Murphy Sculpture Garden, UCLA

INTRODUCTION

How can you possibly write a book about museums and galleries in Southern California when there's so little to discuss?—A friend from New York

It is a myth that the Big Orange is a lemon when it comes to culture. Southern California has become an important international visual arts center. The sprawl between Santa Barbara and San Diego is studded with museums, galleries, and other visual-art resources which are flourishing in the sun. The impact of these institutions and organizations may be diluted by the distances between them, but taken together they constitute an impressive cultural force.

Southern California's art treasures encompass everything from art of the ancient masters to expressions about contemporary issues. There is not just much to see, but a quality that demands respect. And the energy and outlook that are intrinsically "Southern California" are reflected in the state of the arts. There is a vitality here often missed in cities with more firmly established cultural traditions. The Southern California art community, from venerable museums to avant-garde galleries, benefits from that special exhiliration which comes from being young and fresh and, perhaps, just a little crazy.

HOW TO USE THIS BOOK. *Inside L.A. Art* presents a general overview of museums and galleries in Southern California. Listings are organized into four major sections: museums, non-profit galleries, university galleries, and commercial galleries. Institutions have been classified according to their generic identifications because a cultural institution should be defined by what it presents, not where it is located.

Each section is subdivided into special categories which are presented alphabetically. Specific listings include general data such as hours, telephone numbers, and directions as well as information on public transportation, dining facilities, and wheelchair access. There is a general overview of each organization's philosophy, focus, permanent collections, and exhibition policy. Descriptions about the scope and depth of past exhibitions can provide some clues about future endeavors. The index at the back of this book cross-references each listing alphabetically, geographically, and institutionally.

Art facilities can be rather fickle, and hours of operation can fluctuate according to the mood of the taxpayers, the whims of a director, or the traditions of a particular area. For instance, as more galleries gravitate to downtown Los Angeles, they may synchronize their hours of operation to attract more visitors. And, of course, there is always the possibility that an institution, especially a commercial gallery, will relocate or go out of business. It is therefore wise to call ahead.

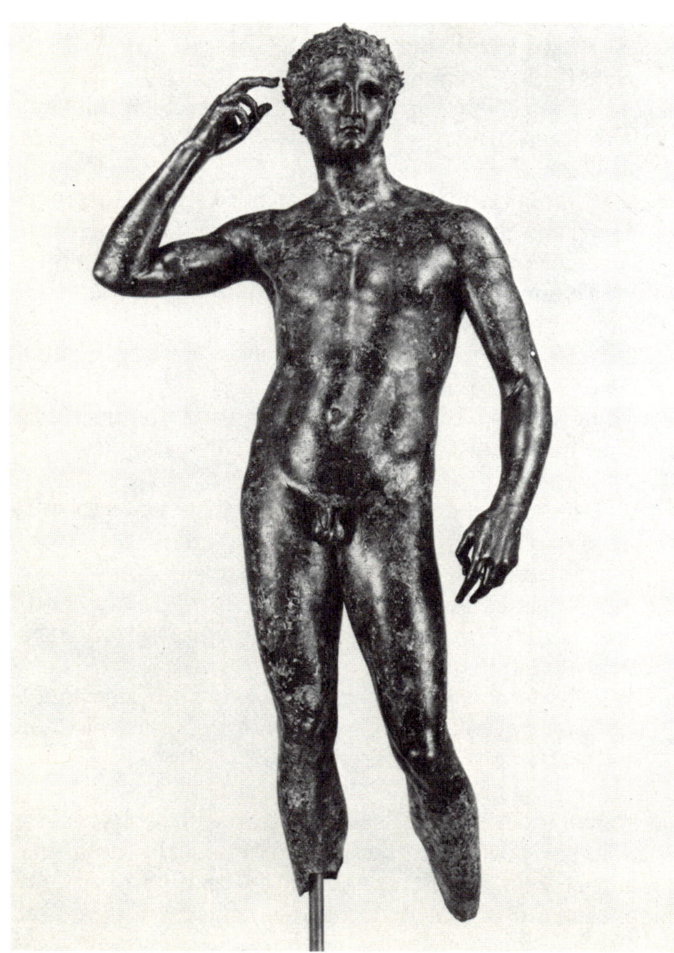

Getty Bronze, Lysippos
J. Paul Getty Museum, Malibu

A museum is an institution which cares for and displays objects of lasting interest and value. Museums house a variety of collections, ranging from art masterpieces to Madame Tussaud's wax creations.

Although this guide concentrates on art, brief descriptions of museums with unique or important collections also have been included. The listings are divided into five major categories: art museums, children's museums, historic houses that operate like museums, special museums, and general museums concerned with natural history and science.

Museums—whether they are concerned with Oriental culture or ornithology—share a number of common characteristics. Major public and private museums are governed by a board of trustees and administered by a museum director, and regardless of their specialization, all museums present permanent and/or temporary exhibitions.

Most museums maintain permanent collections of objects they have acquired by direct purchase or from donations. These objects may be on permanent display, featured in temporary exhibits, kept in a storeroom, or loaned to other institutions. Important exhibits organized by one museum very often travel to other institutions.

A museum's reputation is based on the quality of its permanent collection as well as the scope and depth of its exhibitions, related research, and education programs. The general acquisition, study, and exhibition of objects is the responsibility of curators—art historians, anthropologists, or scientists, as required by the collection. But curatorial concerns tell only part of the story. Museums, especially large institutions, also rely on many professionals who are responsible for the other facets of a museum's overall operation. These include museum education specialists; registrars who are responsible for the inventory, insurance, and whereabouts of every object in a museum; preparators who physically handle the art and install the exhibitions; conservators who preserve and maintain the objects and usually specialize in a particular area such as painting, paper, or textiles; librarians who maintain the research facilities associated with many museums; editors and designers who produce museum publications; photographers who document the collection for publication and research purposes; public information officers who coordinate public relations activities; and the security staff which is responsible for protecting the objects. Those who give tours are called docents, meaning teachers or lecturers. They are usually volunteers. Many museums depend heavily on volunteer support to augment their activities.

But without visitors museums would not need to exist. Scholarly research could be relegated to academic institutions and the objects would become the property of private collectors. Museums make it possible for all people to enjoy and appreciate the historic and artistic expressions of the human experience. And while objects may reside in the collection of a particular museum, they can ''belong'' to no one, since they are the collective wealth and heritage of all of us.

ART MUSEUMS

CHARLES BOWERS MUSEUM

2002 North Main Street
Santa Ana, California 92706
(714) 547-8304 Information
(714) 972-1900 Administrative Offices
HOURS: Tuesday through Saturday, 9 AM to 5 PM, Sunday, 1 to 5 PM
ADMISSION: Free
DIRECTIONS: Located at Main and Twentieth Streets. From the Santa Ana Freeway (south), take the Main Street exit, turn right, and continue for one-half mile to Twentieth Street.
PARKING: Museum lot
PUBLIC TRANSPORTATION: Orange County Transit Line or RTD Line 800
WHEELCHAIR ACCESS: Yes, but flagstones in courtyard may be difficult to maneuver
DINING: None
SHOP: Excellent selection of gift items that relate to museum collections, including masks, ethnic art, rugs, handmade clothing, jewelry, and books
TOURS: Tours by advance reservation. Times and schedules depend on the exhibit. Audio-cassette tours are also available.
FOCUS: General museum with changing and permanent collections on California and Orange County history, natural history, science, and art.

It is unusual to find a small-town museum with an aggressive art exhibition policy, but the Bowers Museum in Santa Ana is just that. It is almost as though the museum has two personalities: one that concentrates on local and natural history, and another concerned with bringing art experiences into the area.

The museum's permanent collection of early California and Orange County history is nicely displayed in the original wing of the museum, a Spanish Mission–style building that looks like a private home but was actually built as a museum in 1932. The Indian Room features Indian artifacts and baskets while the Ethnic Gallery offers a selection of objects from New Guinea and Africa in addition to some very fine pre-Columbian pieces.

In the early 1970s, a new wing was added to display special exhibitions, and the Bowers now mounts about thirty shows each year. Rotating exhibits highlight objects from the museum's natural history collection such as fossils, shells, birds, and plant and animal specimens. The museum also has permanent holdings in Mexican antiquities from Olmec, Aztec, and Mayan civilizations as well as a large antique doll collection. Art exhibits tend to be of an historic nature.

Recent shows have included major sculptural works of the late American sculptor Gaston Lachaise; ''The Oriental Rug as a Work of Art;'' ''Tunisian Mosaics;'' ''Survival: Life and Art of the Alaskan Eskimo;'' ''Egyptian Fayum Mummy Portraits;'' ''Paintings from the J. Paul Getty Museum Collection;'' ''The Gund Collection of Western Art;'' ''Treasures from Cypress;'' ''Russian Icons;'' and ''Paintings on Vases in Ancient Greece.''

The Bowers Museum also has a unique mobile museum that takes a variety of exhibits to Orange County schools.

CONEJO VALLEY ART MUSEUM

197 North Moorpark Road, Suite E
Thousand Oaks, California 91360
(805) 495-3253
HOURS: Tuesday through Sunday, noon to 5 PM; Friday, noon to 9 PM
ADMISSION: Free
DIRECTIONS: Take the Ventura Freeway (west) to Moorpark Road exit; the museum in located in Janss Mall.
PARKING: In shopping mall
PUBLIC TRANSPORTATION: RTD Lines 123 and 161
WHEELCHAIR ACCESS: Yes
DINING: None
SHOP: Selection of gift items, catalogues, folk art, contemporary crafts, and fine toys.
TOURS: Arranged for groups.
FOCUS: Changing art exhibitions.

The Museum serves a population otherwise quite removed from exhibitions of high caliber. In the day of gas shortage and energy saving, the museum places art directly into the mainstream of community life where both seasoned museum-goers and novice appreciators can enjoy the discoveries of art.—Conejo Valley Art Museum Publication

This small museum was among the first to reap the benefits of being located in a shopping complex. Established in 1977, the Conejo Valley Art Museum in a true community musuem which brings a variety of art experiences to a general audience.

Recent exhibitions have featured ''Navajo Chiefs' Blankets and Prehistoric Indian Pottery;'' ''Walker Evans Photographs;'' ''Works on Paper by Los Angeles Artist Billy Al Bengston;'' ''California Horizons,'' which featured landscape paintings of the 1920s; "Indonesian Textiles;" "Arthur Dove;" "New Monotypes by Ed Moses;" "Four American Photographers: Ansel Adams, Alfred Stieglitz, William Eggleston and Roderick Bradley;" and an exhibit that featured the work of contemporary artists John Okulick, Gwynn Murrill, and Robert Bassller.

Although the Conejo Valley Museum exhibits probably don't attract visitors from Los Angeles (the Arthur Dove exhibit was a major exception), the museum provides a valuable service to the community of Thousand Oaks by presenting excellent art exhibits in an accessible location.

THE CRAFT AND FOLK ART MUSEUM

5814 Wilshire Boulevard
Los Angeles, California 90036
(213) 937-5544
HOURS: Tuesday through Sunday, 11 AM to 5 PM; Friday
    until 8 PM
ADMISSION: Free
DIRECTIONS: Located across the street from the Los
    Angeles County Museum of Art, the Page Natural
    History Museum, and the La Brea Tar Pits. From the
    Santa Monica Freeway take the Fairfax exit (north)
    and turn right on Wilshire Boulevard.
PARKING: Small lot adjacent to the museum. Ample street
    parking.
PUBLIC TRANSPORTATION: RTD Line 83 (Wilshire Boul-
    evard) on Wilshire at Curson, RTD Line 89 (Fairfax
    Avenue) on Fairfax at Wilshire, and Line 877 (Culver
    City-Robertson Boulevard-Hollywood) on Fairfax at
    Wilshire.
WHEELCHAIR ACCESS: Poor. No access to restaurant,
    upper gallery or restrooms.
SHOP: Since the museum started out as a gallery, the shop
    retains that flavor in quality and display, specializing in
ceramics, jewelry, and other hand-made objects. There is a nice selection of books.
DINING: The Egg and the Eye Restaurant, one of the finest museum eating facilities. Menu features fifty-four tantalizing omelettes in addition to salads, desserts, and a full bar. Open evenings when the museum is closed. Moderately expensive.
TOURS: Half-hour docent tours scheduled every Tuesday, Thursday and Saturday at 1:30 PM. Depending on the exhibition, tours can range from highlights to informal gallery walks.
FOCUS: Changing exhibits of contemporary crafts and folk art.

More and more people are searching for alternatives to the styles of mass production. Surrounded by synthetic products of the machine age, they find meaning in the straightforward work of folk artists and contemporary craftsmen.—CAFAM Publication

The Craft and Folk Art Museum (CAFAM) has established a well-earned reputation for creative and unique programs that celebrate man's artistic creations. The museum exhibits, preserves, and teaches folk and handicraft traditions, and also provides a place for contemporary crafts people to display their work.

CAFAM evolved from a commercial gallery and restaurant—The Egg and the Eye—which was created in 1965 by Edith Wyle. Way ahead of its time, The Egg and the Eye sponsored exhibits, featured visits to craftsmen's studios, and offered lectures, classes, and films on folk art and contemporary crafts. It conducted itself like a museum but had to operate like a commercial gallery. In 1976, The Egg and the Eye was reclassified as a nonprofit institution and emerged as the Craft and Folk Art Museum. Since then, it has demonstrated a vitality and excitement as its commitment to crafts and folk art expands.

The museum, which organizes five or six exhibits per year, has but two galleries. Despite the limited space, the galleries rarely seem cramped, and they provide an intimate atmosphere as well as an appropriate scale for viewing items. Folk art exhibits are usually installed quite ingeniously, and every effort is made to create a sense of the place from which the objects came. For instance, an exhibit of Greek folk art was displayed against backdrops that recreated a Greek Village. Music is sometimes played in the gallery to enhance an exhibit. Past exhibits have included: "Weaving Traditions of Highland Bolivia;" "Wind and Weathervanes;" "Akari Light Sculpture by Isamu Noguchi," which was featured simultaneously with "Traditional Japanese Toys;" and "Four Leaders in Glass."

FESTIVAL OF MASKS. The Festival of Masks, an annual two-day event held the last weekend in October, is an exciting celebration of different cultural heritages using the tradition of the mask, a universal image. The Festival—held across from CAFAM in Hancock Park—features ethnic entertainment and booths serving international cuisine, and culminates in a Parade of Masks down Wilshire Boulevard. The Festival started in 1976 and is co-sponsored by the Los Angeles County Department of Parks and Recreation.

GALLERY THREE. CAFAM recently opened an annex space, Gallery Three, which will focus on contemporary crafts. It is located at 393 Santa Monica Place, a new shopping complex in downtown Santa Monica.

DOWNEY MUSEUM OF ART

10419 South Rives Avenue
Downey, California 90241
(213) 861-0419
HOURS: Wednesday through Sunday, noon to 5 PM
ADMISSION: Free
DIRECTIONS: Located in Furman Park. Take the Santa Ana Freeway (south) to Paramount exit and turn right. Turn right on Florence Avenue and then left on South Rives.
PARKING: Adjacent lot
PUBLIC TRANSPORTATION: From downtown Los Angeles, RTD Line 800 or 802 stops at Paramount and Florence, two blocks from the museum.
WHEELCHAIR ACCESS: Yes
DINING: None
SHOP: Some art periodicals and gift items.
TOURS: Docent tours are available for groups by advance arrangement.
FOCUS: Changing exhibits with an emphasis on contemporary art.

The Downey Museum's small but rich permanent collection of contemporary California art is something of a surprise to find in the southeast Los Angeles area.

The museum's permanent collection, showcased in a series of changing exhibitions, features work from the 1920s to the present. Artists include Billy Al Bengston, Corita Kent, Don Emery, Sabato Fiorello, Anna Mahler, Shirley Pettibone, and Betye Saar, as well as a number of major Southern California photographers.

Established as a private museum in 1957, the five-gallery museum presents a variety of other temporary exhibits designed to enrich the twenty-seven communities in the immediate area. Past exhibits have included "Rembrandt Etchings;" "Navajo Rugs and Indian Chiefs' Blankets," which was an historical survey of antique and contemporary American Indian weaving designs; and "Configurations," featuring four local artists working in different media.

EDWARD–DEAN MUSEUM OF DECORATIVE ARTS

Riverside County Art and Culture Center
9410 Oak Glen Road
Cherry Valley, California 92223
(714) 845-2626
HOURS: Tuesday through Saturday, 10 AM to 5 PM; Sunday, 1 to 5 PM; closed two weeks following Labor Day
ADMISSION: $1.00 for adults; 50¢ for senior citizens
DIRECTIONS: Take Highway 60 to Beaumont Avenue north. Drive for five miles and then turn left on Oak Glen Road. From Redlands-San Bernardino (10) take Cherry Valley and turn off to Beaumont Avenue (north).
PARKING: Yes
WHEELCHAIR ACCESS: Yes
PUBLIC TRANSPORTATION: No
DINING: None. No picnics allowed.
SHOP: The Sales Gallery features the work of local artists, and a sales counter sells slides and small objects.
TOURS: Docent tours available throughout the day and by advance arrangement.
FOCUS: Permanent collection of European decorative arts; changing exhibits of local art in the North Gallery.

The eclectic approach of the founders of the museum is shown by their selection of furnishings and accessories of many different periods and styles, combining the formal with the informal, the ornate with simple and blending the whole into a harmonious environment.—Guidebook to the Edward–Dean Museum of Decorative Arts

A visit to the Edward–Dean Museum of Decorative Arts is like going to see two wonderfully eccentric uncles who live in the country. The museum is situated on sixteen acres of landscaped parkland, including a cherry orchard, and driving through the countryside of Cherry Valley, a small community in the foothills of the San Bernardino Mountains, is a delight.

The eight-room museum, operated by the Riverside Department of Parks, is the gift of J. Edward Eberic and Dean W. Stout, two men whose passion for antique collecting resulted in a wonderfully eclectic and, at times, quite excellent mélange of European furniture, clocks, small sculpture, porcelain, tapestries, and paintings. Once in the museum, one can sense the exuberance of Eberic's and Stout's collecting—one can feel their presence in every gallery and take delight in their love of the unusual.

Although the museum has the feel of a home, it was built specifically to house the collection. Eberic's and Stout's private residence, first used as a weekend retreat, is adjacent to the museum and features a sales gallery of work by local artists. The two men, who were partners in an antique business, built the gallery to display their collection and opened it to the public in 1958. The museum and grounds were deeded to Riverside County in 1964.

Unlike most museums, the Edward–Dean does not rope off its displays; entering each gallery is like walking into a room in someone's private home. It is possible to go up to a china cabinet and examine all the treasures it contains, from fascinating paperweights to tiny gold cases called vinaigrettes which held cotton soaked in ammonia to revive fainting ladies.

Each room contains a variety of wonderfully unrelated objects. For instance, in the Pine Room one finds a Waterford crystal chandelier; Sir Peter Lely's portrait of Anne, daughter of the Earl of Rochester; pine paneling carved at Grindling Gibbons in the seventeenth century (the companion staircase, the museum proudly notes, is on exhibit at the Metropolitan Museum in New York); Tibetan and Chinese gilded bronze figures; and porcelain and pottery by Meissen, Wedgewood, and Spode. In the Oriental Room, there are twelve Japanese scrolls, an English Regency Chair (one of a set of twenty-four made for Lord Nelson), a sixteenth-century Italian *cassone* (wooden chest), and a bronze statue of Icarus by Bernevitz (1903).

The museum's lower level, which houses a reference library, rare books, and manuscripts, also features displays of old glass, Capi di Monte vases, Wedgewood basalt busts, and an Albrecht Dürer etching, dated 1566.

THE FRANCIS E. FOWLER, JR., MUSEUM

9215 Wilshire Boulevard
Beverly Hills, California 90212
(213) 278-8010
HOURS: Monday through Saturday, 1 to 5 PM
ADMISSION: Free
DIRECTIONS: Located on Wilshire Boulevard between Maple and Palm Drives, east of Beverly Drive. From the Santa Monica Freeway, take the Robertson Boulevard exit (north) to Wilshire; turn left, and the museum is on the right.
PARKING: Lot behind the museum; metered street parking.
WHEELCHAIR ACCESS: Good. Park behind the museum; one-story building.
PUBLIC TRANSPORTATION: RTD Line 83 (Wilshire Boulevard) on Wilshire at Palm.
SHOP: None
DINING: None
TOURS: No public tours; group tours by special arrangement.
FOCUS: Permanent collection of decorative arts objects from Europe and Asia.

Behind its misleadingly bland, modern facade, the Francis E. Fowler Museum is a jewel box glimmering with silver, gold, gems, and ivory. The eclectic collection features twenty categories of decorative arts objects from Europe and Asia. Highlights include a dazzling selection of silver, rare carved ivories, firearms, ship models, snuff bottles, glass paperweights, and various other strange and lovely *objets d'art.*

The entire collection of some six thousand objects was assembled by Francis E. Fowler, a corporate executive who made his fortune in the insurance and liquor industries. There is no common thread to the collection, except perhaps a love of objects that are rare, elaborate, and priceless. There is no doubt that Mr. Fowler also was in love with the art of collecting.

The Fowler Collection is distinguished for the quality and variety of its English, Early American, and Continental silver. The museum's English silver spans four centuries and includes pieces made by such notable silversmiths as Thomas Bampton, John Ruslen, Robert Cooper, George Garthorne, Paul de Lamerie, Gabriel Sleath, William Grundy, Benjamin Smith, and Paul Storr. Early American silversmiths are represented by such masters as Paul Revere, John Coney, Adrian Bancker, John and Benjamin Burt, and Nicholas Roosevelt.

Among the Fowler treasures are objects that belonged to famous historical figures: the "Rasputin Chalice," a gilt-silver vessel adorned with precious gems that was a personal gift from Tsarina Aleksandra Fyodorovna to the mysterious court figure, Rasputin; Oliver Cromwell's "blackjack," a leather drinking vessel with silver mounts; and from the daughter-in-law of President John Quincy Adams, a silver egg-warmer.

Because a fair number of the objects belonged to royalty and the aristocracy, the collection offers a fascinating glimpse into their extravagant spending and elaborate lifestyles. The objects are examples of the finest craftsmanship of the time and were made of the most valuable and precious materials available.

THE J. PAUL GETTY MUSEUM

17985 Pacific Coast Highway
Malibu, California 90265
(213) 454-6541 Information/Reservations
(213) 459-2306 Administrative Offices
HOURS: Tuesday through Saturday (mid-September through mid-June), 10 AM to 5 PM; Monday through Friday (summer schedule), 10 AM to 5 PM
ADMISSION: Free
RESERVATIONS: Advance parking reservations are advised for guaranteed parking and admission. Reservations are free and may be requested by calling the museum or writing in advance. (Specify the specific date and whether morning or afternoon arrival is preferred.) Visitors arriving by car without a reservation are admitted only if parking is available; the museum does not allow visitors to park outside and walk in. Visitors arriving by taxi, bicycle, or public bus do not need a reservation.
DIRECTIONS: One mile north of Sunset Boulevard and 4/5-mile south of Topanga Canyon Boulevard. The Santa Monica Freeway (west) merges with the Pacific Coast Highway and can be taken directly to the museum.
PUBLIC TRANSPORTATION: RTD Line 175 stops in front of the museum but it is a long walk up a steep cobblestone road to the museum. Bus passengers must ask the driver for a museum pass.
WHEELCHAIR ACCESS: People in wheelchairs have access to all the galleries but cannot reach the gardens or Tea Room.
SHOP: The Getty Bookstore is very small but offers a good selection of books relating to the collections. Reproductions and slides of objects in the collection are available, and the museum publishes an annual datebook and an address book.

DINING: The Garden Tea Room serves a cafeteria-style lunch from 10:30 AM to 2:30 PM and desserts and beverages until 4:30 PM—moderately priced and in a nice setting. (Wine and beer are available.)
TOURS: Orientation docents offer free introductory lectures every 15 minutes in the main garden. Spotlight lectures on various facets of the museum are given throughout the day. Audio-cassette tours may be rented from the bookstore.
FOCUS: Permanent exhibitions of Greek and Roman antiquities, Western European paintings, and French decorative arts.

The J. Paul Getty Museum is testimony to one man's creativity, vision, and money.

Oil billionaire J. Paul Getty (1892–1976) established the Getty Museum in 1953 as part of his large Spanish-style house in Malibu, but in the mid-1960s he decided that a larger building was needed to accommodate his rapidly growing collection. He chose to model the new museum after a classical building, the Villa del Papiri. Four years and seventeen million dollars later, the new museum opened. Although Getty, who lived in England until his death, never visited the museum, he left the bulk of his immense estate to it. Today, it has the distinction of being the richest museum in the world.

THE BUILDING. Getty wrote, ''I thought it worthwhile to create one building in the Roman tradition. The Greco-Roman buildings that remain to us have had hard usage during the last couple of thousand years. I suppose that 99.99 percent of the buildings of Imperial Rome have disappeared. . . .'' Getty wanted to re-create an ancient building as it would have existed in its prime, not as a nostalgic ruin. People were surprised—they expected to find crumbling walls softened by time. They did not expect or consider that at one time all the ancient buildings were brand new, their highly polished marble and brightly colored walls glinting in the Italian sun.

Dubbed "Gettyland" when it first opened in 1974, the museum building is an authentic re-creation of a first-century B.C. Roman country house, the Villa del Papiri, which stood outside the city of Herculaneum in southern Italy, overlooking the Bay of Naples. In 79 A.D. when Vesuvius erupted and destroyed Pompeii, the villa was totally buried under tons of volcanic mud. It was forgotten for centuries until, in 1750, monks sinking a well in a monastery garden accidentally hit an exquisite circular marble floor which led to an underground villa. A treasure hunt, financed by the Bourbon king of Naples, explored the villa via underground tunnels—and since the villa was under sixty feet of hardened volcanic rock, this was no easy task. Although the tunnels have since caved in, leaving the villa deep underground, a floor plan and notes made during the excavations provided the basis for the Getty Museum building.

You may not like what you see—the Romans were not known for their subtle taste—but all of the colors and designs in the building are re-creations of what existed in ancient Rome. All of the architectural details in the museum building are derived from ancient specifications, with the exception of modern building-code requirements, elevators, electricity, and other twentieth-century conveniences.

The bright, illusionistic wall paintings in the gardens are based on ancient frescoes, and the colors were matched to authentic samples; the marble floors and elaborate ceiling are copies of those found in the ancient villa; and the bronze statues in the gardens are casts of statuary found in the villa during the eighteenth-century explorations. (The originals are in the Naples Museum.) The original villa, which received its name from a library of papyrus that was found during the explorations, was surrounded by beautiful gardens. The Getty, as part of its re-creation, includes gardens that feature the same types of trees, flowers, shrubs, and herbs that might have been growing two thousand years ago in southern Italy.

The building is remarkable, as was Getty's idea to use a classical building for his collection. And, most importantly, it creates a delightful and appropriate environment in which to view the antiquities collection.

THE COLLECTIONS. The museum concentrates on three specific areas: Greek and Roman antiquities, Western European paintings, and French decorative arts. There is no particular reason for these three specific collections except that Mr. Getty was fond of the periods of history they represent.

Antiquities—Main Floor. This collection, considered one of the three most important in the United States (the Metropolitan in New York and Boston's Fine Arts Museum are the other two), concentrates on marble and bronze sculptures but also includes mosaics, vases, terra-cotta figures, Fayoum (mummy) portraits, and fresco fragments. It is especially strong in the areas of fourth-century Attic stelae (grave reliefs) and in Greek and Roman portraits.

According to the Museum's guidebook, "It should be emphasized that most Greek statuary survives only in Roman copies, which date largely from the first centuries after Christ. Many of them reproduce the general appearance of the lost Greek originals, although few can claim a comparable artistic level. The copyists were artisans of varying degrees of skill who sometimes achieved true technical virtuosity; rarely, though, did they work with any real understanding for the essence of Greek art." It is for this reason that the jewel of the antiquities collection is the fourth-century B.C. "Getty Bronze," a magnificent life-sized statue attributed to Lysippos, the court sculptor to Alexander the Great. The only known original by this master, the statue was lost in an ancient shipwreck and found some two thousand years later, in the early 1960s.

Other major works in the antiquity collection include a head by Skopas (350 B.C.) from the west pediment of the temple of Athena Alea in Tegea; an archaic relief (530 B.C.) from Attica that depicts a warrior bandaging the head of a comrade; and three almost life-sized terra-cotta statues of Orpheus and the Sirens from the end of the fourth century B.C.

Decorative Arts—Upper Level. After seeing these impressive galleries you may conclude that there is no question as to why Marie Antoinette was sent to the guillotine. The collection is a testimony to the ostentatious excess of eighteenth-century France, and it features one of the finest collections of eighteenth-century French decorative arts in the United States.

Decorative arts is a category which encompasses furniture, carpets, clocks, tapestries, chandeliers, and small objects, including candlesticks and porcelain pieces. The items in the collection were made for the French nobility and the royal household between the years 1670 and 1790, a period that ranges from the early years of the reign of Louis XIV to the French Revolution. Although the collection is not large, the quality is unsurpassed. Some of the objects are displayed in paneled rooms of the period which feature authentic floors and wall treatments.

When looking at some of the more bizarre pieces, it is helpful to (a) remember the history they reflect and (b) carefully examine the objects' details to appreciate the exquisite materials and incredible craftsmanship. Most of the objects in the decorative arts collection were made by master craftsmen of the period. Among these was André-Charles Boulle, the most famous royal cabinetmaker at the turn of the seventeenth century, who perfected the Italian technique of veneering wood with tortoiseshell, brass, and pewter.

Other major craftsmen include Joseph Baumhauer, a well-known cabinetmaker who provided furniture for the Duc d'Aumont and the royal family; Charles Cressent, who was the cabinetmaker to Phillipe Duc d'Orleans, Regent of France; Jean Henri-Riesener—a royal cabinetmaker; Jean-Francois Oeben; and Bernard Van Risenburgh, the most renowed cabinetmaker of the rococo period. (The museum houses eleven pieces by this master.)

The Getty also has a number of fine tapestries and a selection of porcelain produced at the Sèvres Manufactory, which was known for making pieces of unusual colors and shapes.

Paintings—Upper Level. All major schools of western art from the late thirteenth to the early twentieth century are represented in the painting galleries. The main emphasis, however, is on Renaissance and Baroque art of the fifteenth through the eighteenth centuries. Getty's original collection concentrated on sixteenth-century Italian paintings (the High Renaissance) and the seventeen-century Netherlandish paintings (Dutch and Flemish). Although it is not a dazzling collection overall, it does have a number of exceptional masterpieces. The collection, displayed in galleries lined with vivid hues of damask, includes works by Rogier Van der Weyden, Raphael, Rembrandt, Rubens, Georges de la Tour, Veronese, Gainsborough, Boucher, Van Dyck, Gentile da Fabriano, Carpaccio, Masaccio, Canaletto, and Alma-Tadema.

Although the Getty's major emphasis is on its permanent collection, the museum sometimes presents special exhibitions. Recent shows have included a New York collection of Rembrandt etchings, Goya etchings, and a photographic presentation of restoration activities in Venice, Italy.

HEBREW UNION COLLEGE SKIRBALL MUSEUM

3077 University Avenue
Los Angeles, California 90007
(213) 749-8611 or 749-3424
HOURS: Tuesday through Friday, 11 AM to 4 PM; Sunday,
    10 AM to 4 PM; closed Monday, Saturday, and holidays
ADMISSION: Free
DIRECTIONS: Located at the corner of 32nd and Hoover
    Streets near the University of Southern California,
    across from the Shrine Auditorium. Easily reached
    from the Santa Monica Freeway, Hoover exit (south).
PARKING: Large lot behind the museum
PUBLIC TRANSPORTATION: RTD Line 176 and several
    others, including 84 and 5F
WHEELCHAIR ACCESS: Good. Special parking near en-
    trance; museum is a one-story structure.
SHOP: Probably the most extensive collection of Jewish
    ceremonial objects in Los Angeles. Handcrafted items,
    fine quality jewelry (much of it from Israel), books on
    Jewish history, notecards featuring objects from the
    collection.
DINING: None
TOURS: Free docent tours offered every Tuesday and Sun-
    day at 1:30 PM. Tours for groups of ten or more may
    be arranged by calling 749-3424.
FOCUS: Permanent and changing exhibits focusing on Jew-
    ish history, ceremony, and art.

*Who are these people, the Jews? Where did they come
from? How did their character emerge? How have they
endured these thousands of years? How could they out-
live Egyptians, Canaanites, Sumerians, Akkadians,
Amoites, Babylonians, Hyksos, Hittites, Assyrians, Chal-
deans, Dorians, Cypriots, Ionians, Phoenicians, Philis-
tines? These ancient cultures are all dead, almost lost to
memory. But the ancient people of the Bible live today.*—"A Walk Through the Past," Catalogue of the
Skirball Museum

The Skirball Museum offers an opportunity to explore the
rich culture and heritage of the Jewish people. And while it
has a definite point of view, the Skirball uses various aspects
of the Jewish past to illuminate many periods in man's history. People of different faiths will not feel uncomfortable
or alienated, and certainly will come away from their visit
with a deeper understanding of the Jewish culture and its
impact on western civilization.

Dedicated to Mr. and Mrs. Jack H. Skirball, who were
largely responsible for establishing the museum in 1972, the
Skirball Museum is part of the Hebrew Union College and
concerns itself with teaching, providing exhibits and resources for the community, and "preserving and maintain-
ing a permanent record of the Jewish experience."

The Museum's diverse permanent collection of some
twelve thousand items spans centuries, countries, and traditions. It includes archeological materials from the Near East,
European decorative arts from the sixteenth century, and
fine arts dating back to the Renaissance. The collection of
ancient Israeli artifacts includes items spanning millennia,
from primitive stone tools of the earliest nomadic civilizations to sophisticated ceramic objects of the Roman and
Byzantine periods.

Objects from this collection are featured in two permanent installations: *A Walk Through the Past* and *The Five
Senses Show. A Walk Through the Past* is "an invitation to
traverse the course of Jewish history from the age of the
patriarchs to the talmudic period." It features art and historical objects in thought-provoking displays that are used
to tell a tale of history, religion, literature, and lifestyle. The
first gallery is devoted to archeology, and includes models
and graphic displays explaining excavation systems, site sur-
veys, pottery identification, and other aspects of this field.

The Five Senses Show, primarily aimed at children, showcases fine examples of ceremonial art within a sensory-theme environment. Children are introduced to the ritual art of Judaism through sounds, tastes, smells, textures, and images, all of which play a part in the fanciful design and customary use of Judaic ceremonial art.

There is no such thing as "Jewish style" in ceremonial art, according to museum director Nancy Berman. Ritual objects reflect the artistic style of the period and place in which they were made, although the basic function and design emerges from the object's ritual or ceremonial purpose. For instance, the traditional Hanukkah lamp must have nine lights (usually candles). Whether from Italy, Damascus, or Poland, all Hanukkah lamps have nine lights. But the shape and decoration of the lamp usually reflects the major artistic style of the country in which it was fashioned.

TEMPORARY EXHIBITS. The museum's temporary exhibits relate to Jewish history, but also feature contemporary art that in some way reflects Jewish tradition. One exhibit focused on the elderly Jewish community in Venice, California; others include "Jerusalem: City of Mankind" and "Illustrations of the Bible," featuring works by Chicago-born artist David Bennett.

THE HUNTINGTON LIBRARY, ART GALLERY, AND BOTANICAL GARDENS

1151 Oxford Road
San Marino, California 91108
(213) 681-6601 or 792-6141
(213) 449-3901 (Sunday reservations information)
HOURS: Tuesday through Sunday, 1 to 4:30 PM; closed
   Mondays and the entire month of October
SUNDAY VISITS: Advance reservations are required for
   each visitor. Tickets are free and must be ordered by
mail. (Indicate the number of people in each party and the specific date.) A stamped, self-addressed envelope must be included.
ADMISSION: Free
DIRECTIONS: Twelve miles northeast of downtown Los
   Angeles. From the Pasadena Freeway, take the Ar-
   royo Parkway exit, turn right on California Street and
   then right on Allen Street. From the Glendale Freeway
   (134), take the Orange Grove exit, turn left at Colorado Boulevard and right onto Allen.
PARKING: Ample space within the museum grounds.
PUBLIC TRANSPORTATION: RTD Line 431 (Monday
   through Friday only) on Sierra Madre Boulevard at
   Oxford. RTD Line 432 (Huntington Drive) one-quarter mile south.
WHEELCHAIR ACCESS: Good in the buildings; grounds
   may be difficult.
DINING: None. No picnics permitted.
SHOP: Books, reproductions from the collections, postcards, notepaper, and slides are available in addition to
   a selection of rare plants.
TOURS: Docent tours of the gardens are offered Tuesday
   through Friday at 1 PM. An audio-cassette tour of the
   art collection may be rented on entering the gallery.
   Brochures for self-guided tours of each garden and the
   art collection are a bargain at ten cents.
FOCUS: Permanent collection of European art with an emphasis on British paintings.

There are few places in the world where one can meditate in a Japanese garden, study masterpieces by Gainsborough, receive inspiration from the Gutenberg Bible, examine a Louis XIV carpet, read an original draft of the U.S. constitution, marvel at the genius of a Rembrandt etching, and then return the next day for an equally diverse experience.

The Huntington Library, Art Gallery, and Botanical

Gardens offer this and much more. Each of the Huntington's three areas is distinguished in its own right, but having them together is a remarkable achievement which guarantees that each visit will be an enriching experience.

THE GARDENS. The Huntington Complex was established by railroad magnate Henry E. Huntington (1850–1927), who moved to San Marino in 1902. After building a home on his 550-acre estate (it now covers 220 acres), Mr. Huntington decided to find out which of the world's plants would thrive in Southern California. He acquired specimens from every continent and made tests to determine their possibilities for ornamental use as well as agricultural value. Today, the park-like Botanical Gardens bloom throughout the year. There are nearly a dozen different gardens, each featuring a single plant family or emphasizing a single environment or culture.

Specific gardens include the Camellia Collection with over fifteen hundred different varieties that bloom from late autumn through April; the Shakespeare Garden containing plants and flowers cultivated during Shakespeare's time in England; the Rose Garden featuring the largest collection of tea roses in the United States; the Palm Garden with over two hundred mature specimens; the Japanese Garden, a landscaped canyon on five acres that includes a furnished Japanese house, bonsai court and Zen Garden; and the Desert Garden with hundreds of cacti and other succulents on twelve acres.

THE LIBRARY. The Huntington Library, which first opened to scholars in 1920, is one of the great research libraries in the world and contains a collection of five-and-one-half million manuscripts, 315,000 rare books, and 212,000 reference books primarily in the fields of British and American history and literature.

Although the major portion of the library is restricted to qualified scholars, two hundred of the finest rare books and manuscripts from the collection are on permanent display in the Library Exhibition Hall. These include books and documents marking significant developments in the growth of British and American civilization: the Ellesmere manuscript of Chaucer's *Canterbury Tales* (circa 1410), frequently called the most important and beautiful of all literary manuscripts; a Gutenberg Bible (circa 1455), which is one of twelve surviving copies of the first book printed by means of moveable type; the unsurpassed Huntington collection of early editions of Shakespeare, including the first two printings of *Hamlet*; and first-edition books and manuscripts of such major authors as Shelley, Byron, Franklin, Frost, Thoreau, Fitzgerald, London, and Stevens.

THE ART GALLERY BUILDING. The Huntington Collection is housed in the former Huntington residence, one of the few surviving grand American mansions from the early twentieth century. The house, constructed between 1909 and 1911, offers an opportunity to see craftsmanship and materials no longer available or economically feasible. It also provides a superb glimpse into the lifestyle of the American upper class, and, because many of the objects on display—including the paintings—were originally viewed in private homes, it is a highly appropriate setting for the Huntington's art collection.

THE COLLECTIONS. The Huntington's art collection is devoted primarily to British art of the eighteenth and nineteenth centuries and includes paintings, drawings, sculpture, silver, miniature portraits, ceramics, furniture, and decorative arts. Outside of London, there is no other collection of equal quality or depth.

The collection also includes a selection of eighteenth-century French decorative arts: furniture, tapestries, porcelain, and sculpture. A few Renaissance paintings and a small but distinguished group of Renaissance bronze statues are housed in the library building.

The collection is not static; art works are acquired to enhance or fill out the permanent collection. Two major bequests have added a new dimension to the Huntington's holdings. In 1978, the Adele S. Browning Collection added a comprehensive selection of eighteenth-century French paintings as well as major works by Italian, Dutch, and Flemish artists such as Rembrandt, Canaletto, and Van Dyck. In 1980, the Virginia Steele Scott Foundation donated its American painting collection, which ranges in date from 1745 to 1930 and includes major works by such artists as Feke, Copley, Bingham, Eastmas, Homer, Cassatt, Sargent, Prendergast, and Hopper.

British Portraits. The Huntington has one of the most distinguished collections of full-length British portraits in the world. Although most of these full-length portraits were commissioned by the people they represent and eventually went into their private residences, nearly all of them appeared at the Royal Academy Exhibition, the great annual art show of the late eighteenth century in London. Thus, they were conceived with public exhibitions in mind, which accounts for the grand scale and rhetorical air of many portraits. Artists represented included Hogarth, Gainsborough, Reynolds, Lawrence, Constable, and Turner.

Miniature Portraits. The Huntington's collection of miniature portraits provides a unique look at an interesting fad that flourished in England from the late sixteenth to the early nineteenth centuries. Most of the miniatures were painted in opaque watercolors on vellum or ivory, fitted into a locket or pin, and encased with glass. These portraits, which often commanded the talents of the most distinguished artists of the time, were given as tokens of love and affection.

Drawings and Prints. Selections from the gallery's extensive holdings of British and Continental drawings and prints are featured in changing exhibitions. The Huntington Collection of some six thousand drawings and watercolors includes excellent examples of all phases of British draftsmanship from the early seventeenth to the early twentieth centuries. There is an especially strong representation of artists such as Blake and Rowlandon as well as a fine selection of watercolor landscapes. The print collection emphasizes engravings and woodcuts by Dürer, and Rembrandt etchings. Only a fraction of this collection is on exhibit at one time because of the sensitivity of these two media to light.

Decorative Arts (English and French). Most of the interiors in the Huntington were modeled after French and English rooms of the eighteenth century and provide an appropriate backdrop for the gallery's collection of decorative arts. The objects include furniture, tapestries, and small decorative objects, with a limited selection of porcelain from the Chelsea factory and a small collection of Anglo–Irish glass.

Silver. The Huntington's British silver collection is displayed throughout the art gallery and provides an interesting perspective on the customs and attitudes of the owners (e.g., a spoon designed to dislodge tea leaves from the spout of a teapot).

The objects in the collection range in date from the fifteenth century to the early nineteenth century. The spoons and cups are the earliest utensils in the collection; forks did not come into general use in England until the late eighteenth century.

Sculpture. There are three major sculpture collections in the Huntington collection: late eighteenth-century French sculpture; seventeenth- and eighteenth-century English sculpture with an emphasis on portrait busts; and Renaissance bronze statuettes, a collection particularly rich in the work of sixteenth-century sculptor Giovanni Bologna and his followers. These small bronzes originally were intended for private contemplation on a desk or in the study of a collector.

LA JOLLA MUSEUM OF CONTEMPORARY ART

700 Prospect Street
La Jolla, California 92037
(714) 454-3541
HOURS: Tuesday through Friday, 10 AM to 5 PM; Saturday and Sunday, 12:30 to 5 PM
ADMISSION: $1.00 for adults; 50¢ for senior citizens and children under 12.
DIRECTIONS: From Highway 5, take the La Jolla Village Drive exit and turn right. Turn south on Torrey Pines Road and turn right on Prospect.
PARKING: Street parking
PUBLIC TRANSPORTATION: San Diego Transit buses 14 and 34 stop at the corner of Silverado and Girard Streets, three blocks east of the museum.
WHEELCHAIR ACCESS: Good
DINING: None
SHOP: A fine selection of publications on contemporary art and an interesting assortment of items concerned with contemporary design (jewelry, clocks, small sculptures, etc.).
TOURS: Docent tours that stress "learning how to look" are available.
FOCUS: Changing contemporary art.

A museum exists because of its collection, and its collection generates a museum's activities, which traditionally are preservation and education.—Robert McDonald, Senior Curator, La Jolla Museum of Contemporary Art

Perched on craggy bluffs like a small Mediterranean resort, La Jolla seems an unexpected place to find an important museum of contemporary art.

The La Jolla Museum of Contemporary Art is concerned with all aspects of twentieth-century art and emphasizes developments since 1950. Although the museum occasionally exhibits the work of unknown or emerging artists, it subscribes to the philosophy that nonprofit alternative spaces and commercial galleries are the testing ground for new ideas and concepts, while museums validate and preserve what emerges.

Surprisingly, the museum is better known on the East Coast than in San Diego or even in other parts of California. It has an excellent reputation for presenting international trends in all phases of contemporary visual expression, with an emphasis on minimal aesthetics and reductive art. It does not, as one might expect, have many exhibitions that focus on local art.

PERMANENT COLLECTION. The museum's permanent collection focuses on American art and is recognized for its holdings in the areas of Post-Modernist, pop, minimal, and conceptual art. La Jolla is the first museum outside of New York to be forming a permanent collection of industrial design from this century. The collection of design objects which is on permanent display concentrates primarily on chair design of the last 150 years. Martha Winas, curator of education, writes in a recent museum publication, "Viewing chairs in the context of a museum exhibition isolates them from their function. It places them in a sculptural perspective, allowing the viewer to study visually the varying themes, attitudes and currents of thought that have prevailed in design."

EXHIBITIONS. Each year, the museum presents eight major exhibitions in addition to a number of smaller shows that feature objects from the extensive permanent collection. Approximately half of the major exhibits are organized in-house and then circulated to other museums throughout the country. Recent major exhibits have included "Sol LeWitt," an exhibition organized by the Museum of Modern Art in New York; "Robert Moscowitz Paintings;" "Seven Decades of Twentieth Century Art from the Sidney Janus Collection;" and "New California Views," featuring a portfolio of recent work by twenty California photographers.

THE BUILDING. The museum building, designed in the 1920s by California architect Irving Gill, originally was the residence of Ellen Browning Scripps. It has been renovated to accommodate large-scale contemporary works, and the seven galleries provide an outstanding setting for the exhibits. As an added bonus, the museum offers several magnificent views of the Pacific Ocean.

LAGUNA BEACH MUSEUM OF ART

307 Cliff Drive
Laguna Beach, California 92651
(714) 494-6531
HOURS: Open daily except Tuesdays, 11:30 AM to 4:30 PM
ADMISSION: Free
DIRECTIONS: From Newport Beach, continue south on the Pacific Coast Highway to Cliff Drive. The museum is on the corner. From the San Diego Freeway, use the Laguna Beach exit and turn right at the Pacific Coast Highway.
PARKING: Street parking only
PUBLIC TRANSPORTATION: OCTD Lines 1 and 57
WHEELCHAIR ACCESS: Poor. No access to lower level or restroom facilities.
DINING: None

SHOP: Small selection of general art history, posters, and locally hand-crafted items (primarily ceramics).
TOURS: Docent tours for school groups
FOCUS: Temporary exhibits that highlight, but are not restricted to, California art from 1900 to the present.

During the early, golden, formative years of Laguna Beach, life was what most people dreamed California to be. There were picturesque beachcombers and Chinese fishermen, gatherers of driftwood and shells . . . Through photographs and especially paintings, its beauty and charm became renowned. Painters attracted sculptors, potters and poets . . . Painters in the 20s caught the last views of the golden shores, sparkling coastlines, the fishermen, the colorful mountains and ranch life.—Introduction to the catalogue for the Laguna Beach Museum exhibit, "Southern California Artists (1890–1940)"

As the coastline's pure beauty changed, so did the sleepy village of Laguna Beach and the art it produced. Today, surrounded by Orange County's urban sprawl and dotted with condominium developments, Laguna remains a tourist resort but is no longer a peaceful, idyllic beach town. And the fame of its artists' colony has been replaced by a reputation for producing commercially sentimental seascapes.

In 1918, when Laguna was in its heyday as an artists' colony, the Laguna Beach Art Association was founded "to advance knowledge and interest in art; to maintain a permanent art gallery; to create a spirit of cooperation and fellowship between painter and public." The association operated for fifty-four years before being restructured as the Laguna Beach Museum of Art in 1972. The museum serves as a regional institution concerned with the needs of its community, but still continues the tradition of its former incarnation by highlighting California and Pacific Coast art from the 1900s to the present.

The museum inherited a fine collection of paintings by early California artists, which the association had accumulated through its juried shows. Because of the museum's limited gallery space, objects from the collection are not on permanent display; instead, they constitute temporary exhibits or augment special shows that deal with California art.

TEMPORARY EXHIBITS. The eight or ten major exhibits presented each year highlight California art but are not restricted to this area. Most of the exhibits feature traditional mainstream art, and although the museum makes no claims to being contemporary, it does attempt to show current trends.

Exhibits mounted during the summer generally relate to California artists. One of the museum's most ambitious exhibits was "Southern California Artists 1890–1940," which offered a stunning retrospective of this period. Paintings by Southern California artist William Wendt (1865–1946) were featured in another show, and photography exhibits focusing on historic California are also popular.

Recent exhibits not relating to California art have included "Picasso and Goya Etchings from the Norton Simon Museum of Art;" "Illusionistic Realism Defined in Contemporary Ceramic Sculpture," which presented a broad range of styles and subjects by artists from around the United States; a solo exhibit by German expressionist painter Gabriel le Münter; and "Collector's Eye," which featured European and American works from six private Orange County collectors. Two juried exhibits of local Laguna talent are presented each year.

The museum building, designed in the 1930s for the Art Association, is an uninspiring cross between a private residence and a commercial gallery which, nevertheless, provides a pleasant environment in which to view the exhibitions.

LONG BEACH MUSEUM OF ART

2300 East Ocean Boulevard
Long Beach, California 90803
(213) 439-2119
HOURS: Wednesday through Sunday, noon to 5 PM
ADMISSION: Free
DIRECTIONS: On Ocean Boulevard between Cherry and Redondo. From the Long Beach Freeway, take the Shoreline Avenue exit which winds around downtown Long Beach, and then turn right at Ocean.
PARKING: Street parking only
PUBLIC TRANSPORTATION: Long Beach Public Transportation Lines 2 or 14; RTD Lines 36, 423, 841, 860, and 873.
WHEELCHAIR ACCESS: Fair: access to grounds, and ramp up to first floor. Although second floor cannot be reached, the docents have certain objects they can bring to visitors in wheelchairs.
DINING: None
SHOP: The Carriage House Bookshop and Gallery is located in a refurbished carriage house on the museum grounds. The shop sells art books, unique gifts, clothing, and jewelry. This museum is noted for its photography posters of ballet dancers by Harvey Edwards. A changing selection of crafts and original prints is also available.
TOURS: Docent tours on Friday and Sunday at 1 PM
FOCUS: Changing exhibits and video art.

The Long Beach Museum of Art is housed in a charming wooden cottage perched on a bluff overlooking the Pacific Ocean, and the art it exhibits is as surprising as the artificial "oil islands" which loom on the horizon.

The museum's permanent collection, exhibited throughout the year, concentrates on American art of the twentieth century, with an emphasis on Southern California artists. Temporary exhibitions cover a variety of subject matter and time periods. Recent exhibits have included the work of contemporary Mexican photographer M. Alvarez Bravo; the work of photographer/filmmaker Robert Frank; "Amish Quilts;" "Masks;" and master French drawings from the E.B. Crocker collection. The museum operates, in this sense, like most regional museums, hoping to enrich and entice the local community by bringing in traveling shows.

But behind this traditional facade, the Long Beach Museum quietly functions as a nationally recognized media arts resource center that promotes and supports the exploration of "alternative television," also called video art. According to Kathy Huffman, curator of the museum's video collection, video art developed in the late 1960s when portable video equipment became available. Surprisingly, video art is not produced by media professionals, but by artists who use this medium as a way to explore new visual frontiers. Video art can involve narrative stories, performances (it records them but also is part of their essence), documentaries, and electronic imagery. Video installations use TV monitors as elements to alter the space and make a statement.

The museum presents daily videotape showings that change every six weeks. One major show featured video pieces from Japan. A Video Archive of over six hundred tapes that represent the evolution of techniques in the medium may be viewed by appointment, and video artists with current work in progress can receive technical assistance from the museum's post-production studio facility.

THE BUILDING. The museum building was constructed in 1912 for Elizabeth Milbank Anderson, a New York philanthropist. The two-story wooden cottage supposedly was an exact replica of her East Coast home. From 1926 until 1950, the house was used for various things, including a CPO club for the U.S. Navy. In 1950, it was purchased by the City of Long Beach for a municipal art center, and seven years later it was designated as the Long Beach Museum of Art. Although the old house cannot physically provide an ideal exhibit space, it offers a warm counterbalance to the more contemporary shows. The garden surrounding the house includes a small selection of contemporary sculpture.

LOS ANGELES COUNTY MUSEUM OF ART

5905 Wilshire Boulevard
Los Angeles, California 90036
(213) 937-2590 (Information)
(213) 937-4250 (Administration)
HOURS: Tuesday through Friday, 10 AM to 5 PM; Saturday and Sunday 10 AM to 6 PM; second Tuesday of each month, noon to 9 PM (free day)
ADMISSION: $1.00 for adults; 50¢ for students and senior citizens. Free, second Tuesday of each month.
DIRECTIONS: Located at Wilshire Boulevard and Ogden Drive, two blocks east of Fairfax Avenue and just west of La Brea Boulevard. From the Santa Monica Freeway, take the Fairfax exit (north) and turn east on Wilshire.
PARKING: Free parking in Hancock Park lot off Curson Avenue, one block east of the museum. Metered street parking is available on Sixth Street, one block north of Wilshire.
PUBLIC TRANSPORTATION: RTD Line 89 running north and south on Fairfax Avenue, and RTD Line 83 running east and west on Wilshire.
WHEELCHAIR ACCESS: Visitors in wheelchairs may enter through the Ogden Drive staff entrance on the west side of the museum. Access throughout the museum is good.
DINING: The Plaza Cafe is open from 10 AM to 4:30 PM and until 5:30 PM on Sunday. Service is cafeteria-style.
SHOP: Large selection of gift items, postcards, posters and

books is offered. Needlepoint kits feature objects from the collection.

TOURS: Free highlight tours of the permanent collection begin at the Information Desk in the Ahmanson Gallery at 1 PM Tuesday through Friday, and at 2:30 PM during the weekend. Talks on specific areas are offered daily.

FOCUS: General art history museum with permanent and temporary exhibits ranging from ancient art to contemporary installations.

As a public institution, the Los Angeles County Museum of Art has the obligation to bring to this community as rich a panoply of visual and aesthetic experience as is available in the metropolitan centers of the East.— From a publication for the exhibition "A Decade of Collection: 1965–1975, the Los Angeles County Museum of Art"

The Los Angeles County Museum of Art (LACMA) is a well-respected general art museum that works to display the art of all periods from prehistoric times up to the present—a difficult job for any museum, especially for one that was not an independent institution until 1961.

For nearly fifty years, LACMA was a division of the Los Angeles County Museum of History, Science and Art in Exposition Park, and did not move to its present location in Hancock Park until 1965. Its austere building creates a somewhat chilling environment in which to view art, offering neither the imposing pomposity of an historic edifice nor the challenging impact of great modern architecture.

The museum has two major exhibition structures: the four-story Ahmanson Gallery, which houses objects from the permanent collection and special installations (generally those relating to the permanent holdings); and the Frances and Armand Hammer Wing, in which major exhibitions are presented on the plaza level and contemporary art is exhibited on the second floor. A lovely sculpture garden surrounds the museum and features works by Rodin, Calder, Lieberman, David Smith, and Duchamp-Villon.

The garden originally was a reflecting pool which, due to seepage from the tar pits, had to be drained, encouraging many people to call the already unloved building a dinosaur.

PERMANENT COLLECTIONS. There are eleven curatorial departments represented in the museum, with only a small percentage of each collection on view at any one time. Objects from the collections are featured in temporary exhibitions and in the Curators' Gallery on the plaza level. Here is a brief overview of the depth and scope of those areas represented.

American Art. This collection offers a survey of American art up to 1930, with an emphasis on the Hudson River School of landscapes. About one-quarter of the two hundred objects in this collection are on permanent exhibition. Highlights from the collection include *Cliff Dwellers* by George Bellows, Winslow Homer's *Cotton Pickers, Mother About to Wash Her Sleeping Child* by Mary Cassatt, and paintings by John Copley, Jasper Cropsey, and Sanford Gifford.

Ancient Art. Major collections in this department include Iranian bronzes and pottery, Mongolian bronzes, Byzantine glazed ceramics, stamp and cylinder seals from Syria and Iran, and the William Randolph Hearst Collection of Greek red-and-black figured vases, Greek and Roman sculpture, and Roman and Etruscan jewelry. Approximately forty percent of the four thousand objects in this collection are on permanent display. Highlights in the collection include Assyrian wall panels from Nimrud, a statue of Herakles from the Hope Collection, a Roman sarcophagus, a bust of Artemis, and a statue of Athena.

Costumes and Textiles. None of the twenty-five thousand pieces in this collection are on permanent view; instead, they are featured in a series of temporary exhibitions. Major areas of the collection include Peruvian costumes, Islamic textiles, Indonesian textiles, and twentieth-century costumes with items by important French and American designers.

Decorative Arts. Spanning a wide range of time—from the Middle Ages to the twentieth century—this collection features objects in silver, ceramics, glass and wood that describe the history of art with useful and decorative objects of western cultures. Only a small fraction of the collection's 4,500 objects are on display. Major areas of the collection include silver, Early English porcelain, European quattlebaum (glass), and Italian majolica (earthenware) from the fifteenth through the seventeenth centuries.

European Paintings. Seventeenth-century Dutch paintings, Italian paintings of the sixteenth and seventeenth centuries, and French paintings from the seventeenth and eighteenth centuries are the strengths of this collection. Major works are *Magdalen with the Smoking Flame* (circa 1630) by Georges de la Tour; *Madonna and Child with St. Anne and Infant St. John* (circa 1621) by Rosso Fiorentino; Rembrandt's *Portrait of Marten Looten*; *Pieter Tjarck* by Frans Hals; *Soap Bubbles* by Chardin; *Allegory of Navigation* by Veronese; Guido Reni's *Bacchus and Ariadne*; and *The Holy Family* by Fra Bartolommeo. The extensive Armand Hammer Collection of masterpiece paintings, sometimes on display at LACMA, will be bequeathed to the museum.

European Sculpture. Major areas of this collection, which covers the Renaissance through the nineteenth century, are French and Italian terra-cotta of the seventeenth and eighteenth centuries, French medals from the fifteenth to the early twentieth centuries, and works by Rodin and other nineteenth-century sculptors. Highlights include *Judgement of Jupiter,* a marble relief by John Deare; Jean Antoine Houdon's *Bust of George Washington*; *St. Scholastica* by Ignaz Guenther; a fifteenth-century Neapolitan *Guardian Angel*; a marble lintel relief by Firenico Gagini; and a *Bust of Neptune* by L.S. Adam.

Far Eastern Art. Chinese ceramics and Japanese Edo paintings (1650–1868) are well represented in this collection, which covers arts from China, Japan, Korea, and Southeast Asia. Only a few of the three thousand pieces in the collection are on permanent display. Major objects include a Chinese bronze Ting (ceremonial vessel); a Yuan blue and white plate; and a scroll painting entitled Bamboo by Goshun, founder of the Shijo school of Edo painting. Objects include metalwork, glassware, textiles, ceramics from the ninth through the seventeenth centuries, and manuscript illumination.

Modern Art. This department concentrates on European painting and sculpture from about 1860 to the present, and on American art dating from the 1913 Armory Show. Its collections are located in two areas of the museum: the modern section (1860 to 1970, both European and American) is on the third floor of the Ahmanson Gallery, while art of the 1970s is shown in the Hammer Wing. The strengths of this collection are German Expressionism and contemporary American paintings, especially the works of Los Angeles artists. About twenty percent of the 250 pieces in the collection are on permanent view.

Prints and Drawings. This department collects works from the fifteenth century to the present, with an emphasis on prints by Dürer, sixteenth- and seventeenth-century Dutch and Flemish artists (especially Rembrandt), German Expressionists, American artists, and modern and contemporary periods. The collection, which also has a fine selection of old master drawings, includes over forty-five thousand pieces that are featured in changing installations. The most important works in the collection include *The Bridge at Langlois* and *The Postmas Roulin* by Vincent van Gogh; Ingres' *Thomas Church*; *Enter Herodias* by Thomas Beardsley; Rembrandt's *Christ Presented to the People*; *Adam and Eve* by Albrecht Dürer, *Self-Portrait* by Van Dyck; and *Yvonne de Profil* by Jacques Villon.

The department's study room is open to scholars and students by appointment only.

SPECIAL EXHIBITS. Major traveling exhibits that come to the West Coast usually are presented at LACMA, and the museum also organizes large shows that go to other institutions. Here is a brief list of major exhibitions that have appeared at LACMA: "Vincent van Gogh" (1969), "The Cubist Epoch" (1971), "Impressionist and Post-Impressionist Paintings from the USSR" (1973), "Scythian Gold" (1975), "Masterpieces from the Hermitage" (1976), "Leonardo da Vinci Anatomical Drawings" (1976), "Two Centuries of Black American Art" (1976), "Women Artists: 1550–1950" (1977), "Richard Diebenkorn: Paintings and Drawings" (1977), "Treasures of Tutankhamen" (1978), "From Leonardo to Titian: Italian Renaissance Paintings from the Hermitage" (1979), "Mark Rothko: A Retrospective" (1978), "Romantics to Rodin" (1980), "The Golden Century of Venetian Painting" (1980), and "The Avant-Garde in Russia, 1910–1930" (1980).

THE MUSEUM OF CONTEMPORARY ART, LOS ANGELES

A major contemporary museum is being planned as part of the Bunker Hill redevelopment project in downtown Los Angeles. The 500–700-million-dollar project, bounded by Grand Avenue and Second, Fourth, and Olive streets, will cover 11.2 acres. Under a directive from the Community Redevelopment Agency of Los Angeles, 1.5 percent of the project's total construction costs must go toward building the 100,000-square-foot museum. A private nonprofit corporation will assume responsibility for the collection, development, and ongoing activities of the museum, which is expected to open in the mid-1980s.

MINGEI INTERNATIONAL MUSEUM OF WORLD FOLK ART

University Towne Center
4405 La Jolla Village Drive
La Jolla, California 92038
(714) 453-5300
HOURS: Tuesday through Saturday, 11 AM to 5:30 PM, Friday, 11 AM to 9 PM, Sunday, 2 to 5 PM
ADMISSION: Free
DIRECTIONS: Interstate freeways 5 or 805 to La Jolla Village Drive (east). The museum is located in a large shopping complex.
PARKING: In the shopping complex.
PUBLIC TRANSPORTATION: San Diego Transit Lines 34 (local), 105 (from U.C. San Diego), and 50 (express from San Diego).
WHEELCHAIR ACCESS: Good
DINING: The Towne Center has several restaurants
SHOP: A small counter with postcards, catalogues, and posters from Mingei International exhibits. There also is a special selection of museum-quality folk art aimed at serious collectors.
FOCUS: Changing exhibitions of folk art

Folk arts . . . these are essential arts of people living in all times throughout the world. They share in common a direct simplicity and joy in making, by hand, articles both useful and satisfying to the human spirit.—Mingei International Publication

Displaying the "arts of the people" and being a "place where essential arts of daily life may speak for themselves" is the mission of Mingei International Museum of World Folk Art.

Mingei is a special word for folk arts coined fifty years ago by a Japanese scholar, Dr. Soetsu Yanagi, who observed that many articles made by unknown craftsmen in preindustrial cultures had a kind of beauty seldom created by modern societies. A museum publication explains, "He developed theories regarding the nature of beauty of things which are integrally related to life and born of a state of mind not attached to the idea of beauty or ugliness."

Since there wasn't any word to communicate Dr. Yanagi's insight, he combined the words for people (min) and art (gei) into "mingei." The Mingei Association of Folk Art was later established in Tokyo to continue Dr. Yanagi's work. The Mingei International Folk Museum, while not officially connected with the Mingei Association of Japan, was inspired by the idea that in our world of increasing mechanization and fragmentation, few people "perform an act of total attention, hand, head and heart to make a unified expressive statement in some medium."

Utilizing both museum and private collections, Mingei International presents four major exhibitions each year. Recent shows include "A Cultural Mosaic," featuring the folk arts of Brazil; the work of Keisuke Seriawa, a Japanese artist considered a "living treasure" in Japan; "Rites of Passage," an exhibition of textiles from the Indonesian Archipelago; and "Early American Quilts and Weathervanes."

Objects in these exhibits "reflect the character of their cultures and the individuals who made them in a universal language of line, form and color," according to museum founder Martha Longnecker.

In addition to exhibits, Mingei International's activities include locating, collecting, and documenting historical and contemporary world folk art, and presenting lectures, films, and demonstrations. The catalogues published for each exhibit are extremely beautiful and will, no doubt, become as cherished as some of the folk art they discuss.

It is somewhat ironic that a museum devoted to the purity of folk art is located in the middle of a suburban shopping complex. But the location, donated by University Towne Center developers, offers a unique opportunity to introduce many people to the delights of folk art. After passing scores of commercial stores, walking into Mingei International is like entering a cool, white oasis. The simple installation, stark white walls, and polished wood floors make a superb setting for the objects.

NEWPORT HARBOR ART MUSEUM

850 San Clemente Drive
Newport Beach, California 92660
(714) 759-1122
HOURS: Tuesday through Sunday, 11 AM to 5 PM, Friday evening, 6 to 9 PM
ADMISSION: Free
DIRECTIONS: From the San Diego Freeway (405) south, exit at Jamboree Road, drive for five miles and turn left on Santa Barbara Street, then left again on San Clemente Drive. If you are on the Pacific Coast Highway (south), which can be reached from the Newport Freeway (55), turn left on Jamboree Road and then right to Santa Barbara Street. The museum is located in Newport Center, adjacent to Fashion Island.
PARKING: Ample space in front of the museum.
PUBLIC TRANSPORTATION: OCTD Lines 82, 71 and 61 (none stop directly in front).
WHEELCHAIR ACCESS: Excellent. Special parking provided and easy access throughout the museum.

DINING: The Sculpture Garden Cafe, located in an enclosed area, has the reputation for being one of the best museum restaurants around. Operated by the volunteer Museum Council, it serves quiche, salads, and soups. Wine and beer are also served. Most things are moderately priced.

SHOP: Art periodicals, books, and hand-crafted jewelry and gift items are available.

TOURS: Free docent tours at noon and 2 PM

FOCUS: Changing exhibits of contemporary art.

The Newport Harbor Art Museum concentrates on "the art of our time," which it defines as "art of the past one hundred years, with an emphasis on the art of the last thirty years or so." This is a round-about way of saying that it is a contemporary art museum—a way of making the museum less intimidating, especially to the somewhat conservative community of Orange County in which the museum is located. At this time, the Newport Harbor Art Museum is the only institution in the Los Angeles metropolitan area devoted to exhibiting local and national contemporary art. Established in 1963, the Newport Harbor Art Museum is a privately supported institution and has been in its splendid new building since 1977.

The twelve to fourteen exhibits each year integrate hard-edged contemporary shows with more traditional modern art. Described as being to the "left of LACMA [the Los Angeles County Museum of Art] and right of LAICA [Los Angeles Institute of Contemporary Art]," the museum presents a balanced program of exhibits for a community that will embrace moderately experimental art but is not ready for a steady diet of difficult concepts and radical ideas.

Past exhibits range from modern art masters such as Mary Cassatt, Edward Hooper, and Reginald Marsh to contemporary artists with international reputations such as Robert Rauschenberg, Jasper Johns, Tom Wesselmann, and Frank Stella. As a regional museum, Newport Harbor also recognizes its responsibility to the local art community—one recent exhibit was "Our Own Artists: Art in Orange County."

The exhibit space is organized to create a quiet, unintimidating atmosphere. The museum's education department often develops special worksheets designed to increase visitors' understanding and appreciation of what is on display. A Sunday afternoon "Meet the Artist" program features conversations with artists whose work is being exhibited.

PACIFIC ASIA MUSEUM

46 North Los Robles Avenue
Pasadena, California 91101
(213) 449-ASIA

HOURS: Wednesday through Sunday, noon to 5 PM

ADMISSION: $1.00 for the general public 12 years and over. Free to all on the third Saturday of each month. Discounts for senior citizens groups.

DIRECTIONS: From Los Angeles—take the Pasadena Freeway north until it ends at Arroyo Parkway; continue north on Arroyo Parkway to Colorado Boulevard; turn right on Colorado Boulevard and continue east to Los Robles Avenue; turn left, and the museum is on the right.

From the Ventura Freeway—take the Orange Grove exit to Colorado Boulevard and continue east to Los Robles Avenue.

From the Foothill Freeway west—exit at Lake Avenue; turn left on Lake to Colorado Boulevard; turn right on Colorado; continue west to Los Robles and turn right.

PUBLIC TRANSPORTATION: RTD Line 770 going northbound on Olive Street in downtown Los Angeles goes directly to the museum. In Pasadena, Lines 436 or 440 on Colorado Boulevard and Line 423 on Los Robles stop at the museum.

PARKING: Ample street parking available

WHEELCHAIR ACCESS: Good access to first floor. Steps to second floor. No elevator.

SHOP: A variety of Pacific and Asian fine and folk art objects, antiques and other items can be found in the Collector's Gallery on the upper floor. Rare teas and spices, cooking utensils and cookbooks are available from the Gourmet Gallery. The Bookstore (main floor) has a small collection of publications.

DINING: None, unless you are a member of the museum or with a group. (Special gourmet lunches are prepared for groups by special arrangement.)

TOURS: Docent tours are available to all visitors throughout the day. Groups should call in advance for special tours.

An ingenious *Children's Gallery* contains objects related to the theme of each major exhibit. Some of the objects may be handled by young people under the supervision of a docent, and labels are placed at "kid's-eye" level.

FOCUS: Changing exhibits on the art and culture of the Pacific and Asia.

THE BUILDING. The museum building's authentic Chinese architecture and decorative details complement its programs and exhibitions. Originally the home of Grace Nicholson, the historic building was designed in the early 1920s by Marston, Van Pelt and Maybury. Today the building—the former home of the Pasadena Museum of Art—is designated as a Pasadena Cultural Heritage Landmark and is listed in the National Registry of Historic Places. When the Pacific Culture Foundation established the museum in 1970, it rescued this marvelous structure from conversion into a Chinese restaurant or possible demolition.

Decorative features include green roof tiles from China, lovely bronze dragons, and marble Foo dogs who traditionally ward off evil spirits. The central courtyard features ponds, Oriental landscaping, and walkways that add to the quiet serenity of the museum. As in traditional Chinese gardens, there are no straight walkways, since evil spirits are unable to navigate the zig-zag paths and will fall into the water!

THE MUSEUM. The Pacific Asia Museum is the only institution in Southern California exclusively devoted to the arts and cultures from the Pacific and Asia. This covers an immense portion of the globe including Afghanistan, Pakistan, India, Nepal, China, Southeast Asia, Malaysia, Melanesia, Japan, Tahiti, Hawaii, Australia, New Zealand, and Micronesia.

Four major museum shows are mounted each year. Recent exhibits included "Hang and Tang Mural Painting from the Peoples Republic of China," "The Art of Indian Asia," "Indonesia: The Fabled Islands of Spice," "Captain Cook and the Islands of the Pacific," and "Japan: Day to Day." Monthly rotating shows in a small upstairs gallery feature the work of Asian artists, Asian-American artists in Southern California, or local contemporary artists influenced by Pacific or Asian cultures.

All of the major exhibitions have one common bond: each conveys insight into the culture or civilization represented as well as showing objects that have important artistic merit. Music, unique installations, and special effects—such as the fragrant aromas of rare spices wafted through the galleries during a recent exhibit on Indonesia—are used to enhance each exhibit. Classes, lectures, concerts, and demonstrations are also developed in conjunction with exhibitions. A recent exhibit on Japan, for instance, presented a traditional tea ceremony.

PALM SPRINGS DESERT MUSEUM

101 Museum Drive
Palm Springs, California 92263
(714) 325-7186
HOURS: Tuesday through Saturday, 10 AM to 5 PM; Sunday, 1 to 5 PM; closed June through September
ADMISSION: $1.50; free the first Tuesday of each month. Students and children free.
DIRECTIONS: Once you are in this desert resort, the museum is located off South Palm Canyon Boulevard, between Tahquitz McCallum Way and Andreas Road.
PARKING: Lot adjacent to museum
WHEELCHAIR ACCESS: Good
DINING: None
SHOP: Gift shop features work by California artists, handcrafted jewelry, and ceramics. There also is a natural science bookstore.
TOURS: Docent tours are available Tuesday at 2 PM. Natural science field trips start at 9 AM on Fridays.
FOCUS: Changing exhibitions featuring art in all media, natural history installations, and performing arts.

It may come as a surprise that Palm Springs, a desert resort best known for its celebrities, golf courses, and parching sun, also boasts a noteworthy museum. The Palm Springs Desert Museum has the distinction of being in a community that is the vacation or retirement home for extremely wealthy and influential people, and the museum's Board of Trustees boasts such honorary members as Mrs. Gerald Ford and Mrs. Walter Annenberg. Thus it was possible for the museum, established in 1938, to build its splendid new 5.5-million-dollar building which houses an extraordinary performing arts hall, an art museum, and a natural science wing.

Surrounded by beautifully landscaped sculpture courts where works by Henry Moore, Auguste Rodin, and Marino Marini bask in the desert sun, the building seems to grow organically from the desert sand and rock.

ART EXHIBITIONS. The museum serves two distinct audiences: local residents of the Coachella Valley, and the thousands of tourists who flock to Palm Springs. Each year, the museum presents about thirty-five exhibits. Past shows include "One Hundred Years of American Art," primitive Australian bark paintings, desert paintings (popular with local residents), and one-artist shows (California sculptor Claire Falkenstein was featured in 1980).

Rotating exhibits of graphics, photography, and traditional painting are featured on the museum's lower level, while the four upper-level galleries are devoted to major exhibits. Each October and May, objects from the museum's permanent collection are displayed in all of the galleries.

SAN DIEGO MUSEUM OF ART

Balboa Park
P.O. Box 2107
San Diego, California 92112
(714) 232-7931
HOURS: Tuesday through Sunday, 10 AM to 5 PM
ADMISSION: $1.00 for adults (or $1.50 for admission and a recorded tour). Children 16 and under are admitted free when accompanied by an adult. Free admission on Tuesdays.
DIRECTIONS: Located in the El Prado section of Balboa Park. From Highway 5 (north/south) take the Sassafrass exit. From Highway 163 take the downtown off-ramp.
PARKING: In the park

PUBLIC TRANSPORTATION: San Diego Transit Lines 7 or 7B. From La Jolla, Line 30 (weekdays only) and 34.
WHEELCHAIR ACCESS: Good
DINING: Cafe Rey del Moro in Balboa Park serves lunch, dinner, and Sunday brunch.
SHOP: The Museum Store offers reprints of objects from the permanent collection in addition to books, posters, catalogues, postcards, and gift items.
TOURS: Docent tours are available Tuesday, Wednesday, and Thursday at 10 AM, noon, 1 PM, and 3 PM, and on Sunday at 1:00 PM
FOCUS: General art history museum with a broad permanent collection and temporary exhibitions.

The San Diego Museum of Art has all the characteristics of a solid, general art museum complete with a grand staircase and marble rotunda, and you may have the somewhat intimidating feeling that you should whisper in the galleries.

The building's splendid Spanish Renaissance style is a stately setting for the museum's broad scope of permanent and changing exhibitions. The permanent collection offers an overview of five thousand years of western and eastern art and culture, from Egyptian and pre-Columbian periods to the twentieth century. It has an extremely fine selection of Spanish Baroque paintings, with works by Cotan, Velasquez, El Greco, and Zurbarán. Other major artists in the collection include Coltan, Eastman Johnson, Hals, Bosch, Rubens, Jacques Louis David, Matisse, Braque, and Picasso.

The strength of the decorative arts collection is American furniture and silver.

The museum's enclosed sculpture garden features pieces by Moore, Calder, Zuniga, and Lipchitz. Twelve temporary exhibits are mounted each year, and they run the gamut, from Rembrandt etchings to the ''Art of the Muppets.'' Other recent exhibits include ''Five Centuries of Tapestry,'' ''American Folk Paintings,'' and ''Gold of Peru.''

SANTA BARBARA MUSEUM OF ART

1130 State Street
Santa Barbara, California 93101
(805) 963-4364
HOURS: Tuesday through Saturday, 11 AM to 5 PM; Sunday, noon to 5 PM
ADMISSION: Free
DIRECTIONS: In the heart of Santa Barbara, at State and Anapamu Streets.
PARKING: Several public lots nearby as well as street parking.
PUBLIC TRANSPORTATION: The Santa Barbara Metropolitan Transit Center is two blocks from the museum, making it within walking distance of all busses.
WHEELCHAIR ACCESS: Fair
DINING: None
STORE: A few publications and postcards are sold at the information desk
TOURS: Free docent tours at 1:30 PM Tuesday through Friday, and at 2 PM on Saturday and Sunday
FOCUS: Eclectic permanent collection and changing exhibitions.

Like the seaside town of Santa Barbara, the Santa Barbara Museum is a small jewel that emphasizes quality over quantity. The museum's Spanish-style building was the former Santa Barbara Post Office, and the galleries, while not dazzling in their installation, offer a fine space in which to view the museum's first-rate changing exhibits and objects from the permanent collection.

PERMANENT EXHIBITS. Most of the objects on permanent display were donated by Santa Barbara residents. Permanent exhibits include a small but extremely fine selection of Greek and Roman classical sculpture, the Henry Eicheim Collection of four hundred rare historical Oriental musical instruments, and the Alice F. Schott Doll Collection. A collection of West African art and artifacts is also on permanent display.

PERMANENT COLLECTIONS. Objects from the museum's permanent collection are highlighted in a series of rotating exhibitions that are often augmented with loan pieces from private collections. The exhibits generally have a theme that allows different areas of the collection to be featured. Recent exhibits include ''The Child in Art;'' ''Many Faces of Women: Portraits from the Second Century to the Present;'' ''A Garden's Vanity,'' featuring four centuries of still-life and flower paintings; and ''American Art of the Twentieth Century.''

The American Collection, on display at least six months every year, includes paintings from pre-Revolutionary time to 1950 as well as a selection of American drawings with an emphasis on the twentieth century.

The European Collection features paintings and sculpture from the Middle Ages to the present, including several outstanding Impressionist paintings. European drawings, which range from the Renaissance to the present, include examples by such masters as Carracci, Guernico, Tiepolo, Watteau, Boucher, Degas, Dali, Picasso, and Matisse. A selection from this collection is on view throughout the year.

CHANGING EXHIBITIONS. The museum mounts several major exhibits each year, including one major contemporary show and an annual Christmas exhibit designed for children. Exhibits, which do not necessarily relate to the museum's permanent collection, have included ''George Innes;'' ''Japanese Courtier'' (paintings, calligraphy and poetry from the Fogg Art Museum Collection); ''Attitudes,'' an exhibit of over four hundred contemporary photographs; and ''Canaletto Etchings.''

NORTON SIMON MUSEUM OF ART

411 West Colorado Boulevard
Pasadena, California 91103
(213) 449-6840
HOURS: Thursday through Sunday, noon to 6 PM
ADMISSION: $2.00 for adults, 75¢ for students and senior citizens; $3.00 general admission on Sundays. Admission includes a free fine art reproduction from the collection.
DIRECTIONS: Located at the junction of Foothill (I-210) and Glendale (SR-134) freeways. Use the Colorado Boulevard exit.
PARKING: Ample space in museum lot
PUBLIC TRANSPORTATION: RTD Line 434
WHEELCHAIR ACCESS: Good
DINING: None
SHOP: One of the very few museum shops that could stand alone as a bookstore, this one offers a wide spectrum of general art history, scholarly publications, and books on Oriental art. Catalogues from other museums are also featured. The store has a section of children's books on art, one on architecture, and a fine selection of original prints, etchings, and engravings. There is a small number of posters and greeting cards with reproductions from the collection.
TOURS: Private group tours are scheduled for a substantial fee and on a limited basis. Advance reservations are required.
FOCUS: Permanent exhibitions of European masterpieces, with temporary exhibitions featuring objects from the collection.

On an international scale, it's a simply marvelous museum. The general level of quality is extraordinary.—Sir John Pope-Hennessy, chairman of the painting and sculpture department of the Metropolitan Museum of Art, as quoted in the *New York Times*, February 4, 1980

The quality, scope, and depth of the Norton Simon Museum are unequalled in any museum west of New York City. If you can visit but one museum in Southern California, it should be the Norton Simon. The museum represents two decades of collection by one man—industrialist Norton Simon—and it concentrates on the acquisition and display of masterpiece objects.

The collection includes six centuries of European paintings, one of the largest and finest collections of Indian and Southeast Asian sculpture outside of Asia, and monumental nineteenth- and twentieth-century European sculptures. Within the collection are several "mini" collections, such as a unique group of sixty-nine original Degas bronzes found in the artist's studio after his death; sixty drawings by the seventeenth-century landscape painter Claude Lorrain; a hundred and fifty-nine exquisite watercolors from a 1640s Dutch tulip catalogue, and a comprehensive assemblage of graphic works by Goya, Rembrandt, and Picasso.

A series of temporary exhibits feature objects from the museum's vast and growing inventory of over five thousand works of art. Recent exhibits include Rembrandt etchings, Goya etchings, Ansel Adams photographs, and seven decades of Picasso's work.

THE COLLECTION. The Simon collection is remarkable because there is not just one good example of an artist's work, but several, often providing a unique perspective on an artist's development. The following provides a brief overview of major areas represented in the collection and illustrates the size and quality of the museum's holdings.

Italian. Early Italian works include examples by Guariento,

Filippino, Lippi, and Lorenzetti, and the mid-fifteenth-century *Beauregard Madonna* marble by Desiderio da Settignano. From sixteenth-century Italy, there is Raphael's *Madonna and Child with Book*, and from the eighteenth century, Tiepolo's *Triumph of Virtue Over Ignorance*.

Dutch and Flemish. Major pieces include Rembrandt's *Titus*, *Bearded Man in a Wide-Brimmed Hat*, and *Self-Portrait*, and a distinguished group of Rembrandt etchings. Other masters represented include Frans Snyder, Frans Hals, Vermeer, Peter Paul Rubens, van Ruisdael, and Jan Steen.

Spanish. Spanish artists are well represented by Murillo, Goya, and Zurbarán, including the latter's well-known *Still Life with Lemons, Oranges and a Rose*.

French. Seventeenth- and eighteenth-century French paintings include works by Rigaud, Poussin, Chardin, and Watteau. French masterpieces from the nineteenth and twentieth centuries include pieces by Degas, Monet, Manet, Rousseau, Seurat, Cezanne, Renoir, Gauguin, and van Gogh. Highlights are Matisse's *Odalisque with Tamborine*, Rouault's *The Sirens*, *The Ragpickers* by Manet, and *Mulberry Tree* by van Gogh.

Modern schools of the twentieth century are represented by three fine cubist paintings: Picasso's *Point de la Cité*, Braque's *Still Life with Pipe*, and Gris' *Still Life with a Poem*. The famous Galka Scheyer Collection, left over from the museum's days as the Pasadena Museum of Modern Art, includes the works of the Blue Four German Expressionists—Feininger, Jawlensky, Kandinsky, and Klee—but is not always on complete display.

Indian and Southwest Asia. The crowning jewel of this collection is a tenth-century Indian bronze known as the "Shivapuran Nataraja" which is on display for only ten years because it must be returned to India due to a dispute with the Indian government. The earliest sculptures in the collection are two Indian pillars dated from 100 B.C. The collection is particularly strong in art from Cambodia and Thailand.

Nineteenth- and Twentieth-Century Monumental Sculpture. Displayed in a sculpture garden, this collection includes Rodin's *Burghers of Calais,* Maillol's *The River,* and Moore's *King and Queen.* The sculpture collection covers the period from the 1830s to 1973, but the concentration is on sculpture from France and England. Other artists include Matisse, Lipchitz, Laurens, Brancusi, Giacometti, and Arp.

BUILDING AND HISTORY. The museum's austere geometric building is a contrast to the art it houses; in fact, it is a reminder of the museum's previous incarnation as the Pasadena Museum of Modern Art, an institution that opened in 1969 and was reorganized under Mr. Simon's leadership in 1975 because of financial difficulties. The museum's modern collection has been more or less relegated to storage.

One really disturbing thing about the museum is Mr. Simon's insistence on covering many of the paintings with glass. Although intended to provide security for the art works, the glass results in a most frustrating experience for the viewer, who, attempting to scrutinize an artist's brushstrokes, ends up looking at his own reflection.

SOUTHWEST MUSEUM

234 Museum Drive
Highland Park, California 90042
(213) 221-2163
HOURS: Tuesday through Sunday, 1 to 5 PM; closed Mondays, major holidays, the last two weeks in August, and the first two weeks in September

ADMISSION: Free
DIRECTIONS: Pasadena Freeway to Avenue 34 exit, right on Figueroa Street, left on Avenue 54, right to Marmion Way, and a sharp left to Museum Drive.
PARKING: Parking lot, up a steep driveway, directly at corner of Museum Drive and Marmion Way (easily missed). Limited street parking on Museum Drive. The most interesting way to enter is through the underground tunnel on Museum Drive. The tunnel, lined with dioramas showing scenes of Indian life, culminates at an elevator that transports visitors up several floors to the museum.
PUBLIC TRANSPORTATION: RTD Line 6 (at Marmion) or Line 25 at Figueroa
WHEELCHAIR ACCESS: Poor. Lower and upper levels can be reached, but require complicated maneuvering. To reach upper-level galleries, use staff parking area to discharge passenger; for lower level, use the tunnel and elevator on Marmion Way. Steps connect some galleries.
SHOP: In the lobby near the information desk. Museum sells souvenirs with an Indian flavor, a small selection of silver jewelry, and publications relating to the collection.
DINING: None. Picnic or bag lunches may be eaten on the museum's patio.
TOURS: No tours are given to the general public. School tours are offered in the morning and during some public hours. (Advance reservations required.)
FOCUS: Permanent collection of western Indian arts, handicrafts, and historical objects.

Knowledge of a people's arts provides one key to an understanding of their way of life. It is only when we understand and appreciate the arts that baskets, masks, rugs, pots and other artifacts become spokes-

men for their creators instead of curios to be preserved only because they are strange, rare or lovely.—Andrew Hunter Whiteford, in *North American Indian Arts*

Watching the children at this museum is the key to its magic. Children raised on television clichés of war-whooping Indians are awed and delighted to discover America's native people—to explore their rich cultural heritage, to see how they co-existed with nature, to appreciate their ingenuity and the beauty of their art. This is what the Southwest Museum is all about.

The museum's mint-green walls and endless cases crammed with objects and hand-lettered labels evoke an image of what museums were like before they discovered public relations, flashy displays, and other devices aimed at luring visitors. This unpretentious, almost archaic museum persists like an old dowager unwilling to change her ways. And yet, there is charm and nostalgia that makes each visit an extraordinary experience.

The Southwest Museum, in fact, is the oldest museum in Los Angeles, and since its inception in 1907 it has been entirely supported through private donations. Perched on a hill overlooking Highland Park, the Southwest Museum resembles a large pink monastery.

As its name indicates, the museum is concerned with the southwest portion of the United States. The permanent collection is divided into several major areas: Northern and Northwestern Tribes (including Alaska and parts of British Columbia); Plains Indians (Blackfoot, Crow, Sioux, Cheyenne, Kiowa, Arapaho, and Commanche); Southwest Indians (generally those tribes from Arizona and New Mexico); California Tribes; and Prehistory (focusing on early man). Each area features an incredible number of Indian arts, handicrafts, and historical objects, including beautifully beaded moccasins, ceremonial and daily clothing, pottery, leatherwork, furs, featherwork, textiles (exquisite Navajo weavings), and larger objects such as a full-size buffalo skin tepee, canoes, and wooden totem poles.

The highlight of the museum is the Caroline Boeing Poole Basket Collection (upper floor) which features 2,445 examples of basketry from tribes west of the Mississippi. It is a unique collection that presents a comprehensive survey of the scope and beauty of American Indian basketry. The baskets are arranged according to tribes, each tribe having a distinctive style. Black-and-white photographs of Indians using or making baskets are presented in the display cases. The Basket Wing also includes thirteen marvelous dioramas (almost relics themselves) illustrating domestic activities and the various types of homes of the important basket-making tribes.

CASA DE ADOBE. The Casa de Adobe, located at 4603 North Figueroa, just below the museum, is a replica of a charming Spanish Colonial hacienda from early California (1800–1850). It was built in 1925 and includes two museum galleries as well as all of the rooms one would find in such a house. The furnishings, all original, represent several different periods, as furniture would be accumulated over fifty years by a family living in the house. The Casa is open, free of charge, on Wednesday, Saturday, and Sunday from 2 to 5 PM.

THE TIMKEN GALLERY

Balboa Park
San Diego, California 92101
(714) 239-5548
HOURS: Tuesday through Saturday, 10 AM to 4:30 PM;
    Sunday, 1:30 to 4:30 PM; closed all of September
ADMISSION: Free
DIRECTIONS: Located in the El Prado section of Balboa
    Park, adjacent to the San Diego Museum of Art. From

Highway 5 (north/south) take the Sassafrass exit. From Highway 163 take the downtown off-ramp.
PARKING: In the park
PUBLIC TRANSPORTATION: San Diego Transit Lines 7 or 7B
WHEELCHAIR ACCESS: Good
DINING: see San Diego Museum of Art.
SHOP: None
TOURS: Docent tours are available by advance reservation. Audio-cassette tours may be rented. Free brochures on different facets of the collection are available.
FOCUS: Permanent collection of masterpiece paintings, Russian icons, and French tapestries.

This small museum is one of the best-kept secrets in San Diego. Its permanent collection includes a small but exquisite selection of European and American paintings, Russian icons, and French tapestries. The gallery is named for the Timken Foundation in Ohio, which provides the endowment for the building and operating expenses.

Established in 1965, the Timken Gallery houses the Putnam Foundation Collection, objects collected by two Putnam sisters who lived in San Diego. The building is a severely elegant structure of bronze and travertine with six galleries. Natural light, a welcome relief from the somber artificial light in most museums, enhances the treasures in this wonderful, intimate museum. One can visit the gallery without feeling overwhelmed.

The collection includes major Italian, Flemish, Dutch, and French masterpieces, a selection of American paintings from the colonial period to the nineteenth century; and one of the finest private collections of Russian icons in the United States. There is usually just one example of an artist's work, but each painting is a masterpiece. The following provides a brief overview of some of the artists represented.

In the Flemish School, artists include Petrius Christus, Rogier Van der Weyden (school of), Hans Memling, Pieter Bruegel the Elder, and Peter Paul Rubens. Dutch artists include Rembrandt, Hieronymous Bosch, Frans Hals, and van Ruisdael. Spanish artists are El Greco, Juan Sanchez Cotani, Lo Spagnoletto, Zurbarán, and Goya.

French masters in the collection are Philippe de Champagne, Francois Boucher, Francois Clouet, Jean Honoré Fragonard, Jean Baptiste Camille Corot, and Paul Cezanne. The Italian School is represented by Giotto, Luca di Tomme, Niccolo di Buonaccorso, Carlo Crivelli, Titian, and Veronese. The American paintings in the collection include works by Benjamin West, Winslow Homer, Theodore Robinson, Albert Bierstadt, George Inness, Eastman Johnson, and Frederick Remington.

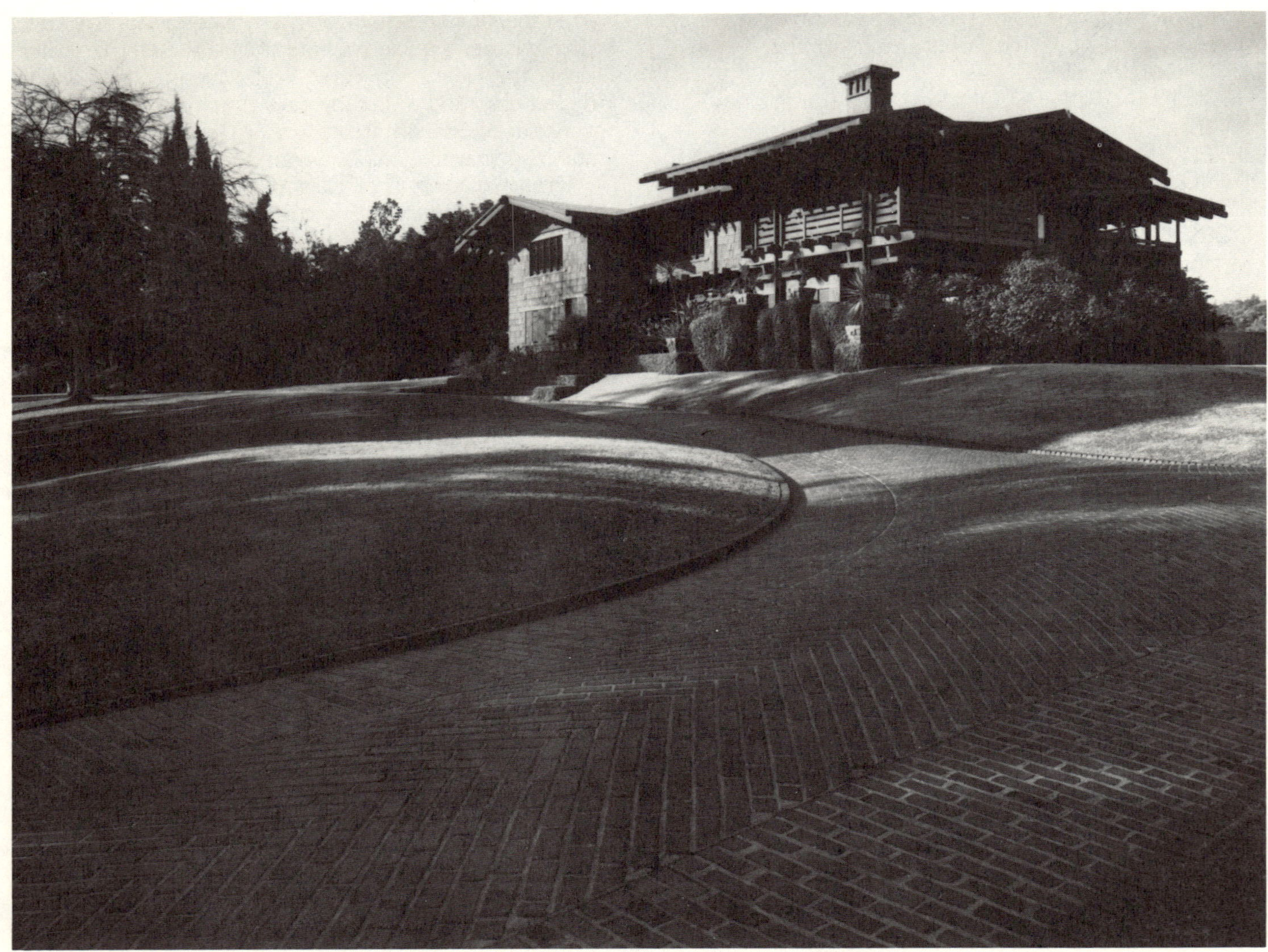

The Gamble House, Pasadena

HISTORIC HOUSES

These three houses, which are open to the general public on a regular basis, are historically and/or architecturally interesting. Historic houses concerned only with regional history have not been included in this guide.

THE GAMBLE HOUSE

4 Westmoreland Place
Pasadena, California 91101
(213) 793-3334 or 681-6427
HOURS: Tuesday and Thursday, 10 AM to 3 PM; first Sunday of each month, noon to 3 PM
ADMISSION: $3.00 per person for admission and tour, which is the *only* way to see The Gamble House. Purchase tickets in the garage.
DIRECTIONS: Situated one-half mile north of Colorado Boulevard (Interstate Highway 134, Route 66), parallel to Orange Grove Boulevard between Walnut Street and Rosemont. Westmoreland Place, a private street, is entered through driveways intersecting the 300 block of North Orange Grove Boulevard.
PARKING: Lot in front of house
PUBLIC TRANSPORTATION: RTD Line 433 or 434
WHEELCHAIR ACCESS: Impossible for wheelchairs.
SHOP: Selection of architecture books.
DINING: None
TOURS: The Gamble House may be visited only via guided tours. The tours are about 1¼ hours long.
FOCUS: Architecture by Greene and Greene, containing objects crafted by the architects.

The building, so beautifully sculpted in wood, is not only a masterpiece of American architecture but importantly attests to the courage of its determined young architects who broke from the training and tradition of their pro-fession to produce one of the few truly American contributions to architecture.—Gamble House Publication

The Gamble House can be considered the Greene and Greene Museum, for it is the most complete and best-preserved example of the work of the internationally acclaimed architects Charles Sumner Greene and Henry Mather Greene. The two brothers, who formed the Pasadena architectural firm of Greene and Greene, are synonymous with the California bungalow and an architectural style that spread throughout the country.

Built in 1908, the remarkable **Gamble House** was constructed for Mr. and Mrs. David B. Gamble (second generation of the Proctor and Gamble family) for $50,000. The house reflects the architects' study of and love for wood, their appreciation for the integrity of Japanese architecture, a respect for the Swiss, and a deep love of natural materials. Interiors feature solid teakwood, maple, and Port Orford cedar, and no detail in the house is overlooked. Every peg, oak wedge, downspout, airvent, opening, and fixture has been designed with the whole in mind. The exquisite Tiffany lamps and specially designed furniture echo the interior and exterior lines of the house. In the living room, Greene and Greene designed the carpets, lighting fixtures, irons and fireplace tools, hardware, and furniture which includes a hand-built piano fashioned in California and sent to the Baldwin Piano Company in Ohio for completion.

Randell L. Mackinson, curator of the Gamble House and professor of architecture at the University of Southern California, wrote in *The Prarie School Review* (Fourth Quarter, 1968):

Nowhere is a detail left to chance. At every turn, one recognizes the unmistakable hand of the Greenes. The integral design of the furniture, lighting fixtures, carpet, picture frames, and hardware blends into the overall composition. Wood paneling and trim are fastened with brass screws covered with square pegs of ebony, mahogany, or oak. Woodwork is detailed so that the various parts come together in different planes.

The Gamble House is jointly operated by the University of Southern California and the City of Pasadena. The Greene and Greene Library, on the premises, specializes in materials on the Greenes as well as related information dealing with the Arts and Crafts Movement, local architecture, and craftsmen of the period. It is open to the public by appointment only.

HERITAGE HOUSE

8193 Magnolia Avenue
Riverside, California 92501
(714) 787-7273
HOURS: Tuesday and Thursday, noon to 2:30 PM; Sunday, noon to 3:30 PM
ADMISSION: $1.00 donation requested (viewed by tour only)
DIRECTIONS: About 10 minutes south of downtown Riverside between Adams and Jefferson. For freeway directions, please see the Riverside Municipal Museum.
PUBLIC TRANSPORTATION: RTD Line 496 (L.A.-Riverside-San Bernardino); or Line 860 (Long Beach-Disneyland-Riverside) to RTD Station at 7th and Market, with a transfer to Line 2.
WHEELCHAIR ACCESS: Only to the first floor
DINING: None
SHOP: A few items made by members of the Riverside Museum Associates are offered for sale.
TOURS: Tours begin about every half-hour.
FOCUS: Restored Victorian home, completely furnished.

Heritage House, owned by the Riverside Museum, is the quintessential Victorian house, complete with a legend about a ghost who periodically haunts her old homestead.

The house, built in 1891 by architect John Walls for Catherine Bettner, looks as though its inhabitants have just departed for a brief carriage ride through the citrus orchards of Riverside and will return momentarily. Until they do, you can—albeit on a tour—poke through the house and discover the odd assortment of objects on display. Similar to most houses of its era, Heritage House is a somewhat overwhelming mixture of many styles, including Queen Anne, Moorish, Georgian, and Chinese. The original wood paneling in most of the rooms, and some of the pieces of furniture—especially in the parlor—are original. This house was one of the first in Riverside to have gas lights, and many of the original gas fixtures remain.

HOLLYHOCK HOUSE

Barnsdall Park
4809 Hollywood Boulevard
Los Angeles, California 90027
(213) 662-7272
HOURS: Tours are given on Tuesday and Thursday at 10 AM, 11 AM, noon, and 1 PM and on the first Saturday and Sunday of each month at noon, 1 PM, 2 PM, and 3 PM
ADMISSION: $1.50 for adults, 75¢ for senior citizens. Children under 12 free.
DIRECTIONS: Barnsdall Park is at the junction of Vermont Avenue and Hollywood Boulevard. From the Hollywood Freeway, exit at Sunset Boulevard and turn east. Turn left on Vermont Avenue and then left on Hollywood Boulevard.
PARKING: In the park

PUBLIC TRANSPORTATION: RTD Line 91 (Hollywood Boulevard). RTD Line 95 (Vermont Avenue-Vernon Avenue).

RTD Line 436 (Hollywood-Glendale-Pasadena) at Hollywood and Vermont. RTD Line 42 (Temple Street) on Fountain near Edgemont.

WHEELCHAIR ACCESS: No

SHOP: None

DINING: None

TOURS: The house can be viewed only by tour. (Tour times are listed by hour.)

FOCUS: House designed by Frank Lloyd Wright

Hollyhock House, the first residence in Los Angeles designed by Frank Lloyd Wright, is an outstanding example of the architect's genius for creating a building for a specific site. Wright, who described it as "a very proud house," told one city official that he "walked through the olive trees and hollyhocks at every hour of the day and night planning the setting, like the Japanese, in harmony with the views and ways of the moon and sun."

Designed for oil heiress Aline Barnsdall in 1919, it is the only Wright house in the city that is open to the public on a regular basis. Miss Barnsdall gave her residence and eleven acres of what is now Barnsdall Park to the city in 1927 with the stipulation that it be used for cultural and recreational purposes; both the Municipal Art Gallery and the Junior Art Center are also located in Barnsdall Park.

Although some describe Hollyhock House as having a Mayan influence, Wright's son, who was a consultant for the building's recent restoration, said his father developed it to reflect a mesa silhouette as originated by the Pueblo Indians.

Today, the house is still remarkable in its design and function. It included a stream that flowed through the garden, disappeared under the house, rose again into the large pool in front of the fireplace, and then disappeared to rise again in outer pools and streams. A large skylight floats over the fireplace, and the strength and simplicity of the house's lines are stunning. Although Wright called it his "California Romanza," Miss Barnsdall always referred to it as Hollyhock House because of the hollyhocks that grew in wild abundance on the property. Wright incorporated an abstract motif of the stately flower into the cast concrete, lamp posts, carpets, and drapes.

It may be difficult to believe, but soon after the house was given to the city, it fell into disrepair and eventually was ordered demolished. Fortunately, Mrs. Forest Murray offered to restore the residence and gardens to their original condition if the city would lease them to her for ten years. Equally fortunate, the city officials could recognize a good deal, and this architectural masterpiece was saved.

Hollyhock House, which is administered by the city's Cultural Heritage Board, presents exhibits that relate to its history. A recent exhibit featured twelve original drawings by Frank Lloyd Wright that were commissioned by Miss Barnsdall as part of the cultural complex which she had hoped to develop on Olive Hill.

CHILDREN'S MUSEUMS

EXPERIENCE CENTER

3531 Main Street
Irvine, California 92714
(714) 552-8228
HOURS: Tuesday through Friday, 9 AM to 4 PM; Saturday
    and Sunday, noon to 5 PM
ADMISSION: Donation $1.00 for adults, 50¢ for children
DIRECTIONS: San Diego Freeway (405) to Culver Drive
    exit; inland to Main Street.
WHEELCHAIR ACCESS: Yes

Patterned after the Exploratorium in San Francisco, the
Experience Center is a participatory science museum in
which visitors explore the world of science and industry
through special exhibits and installations.

The Experience Center, while aimed at children, is a
unique opportunity for people of all ages to learn about the
technology that surrounds them. Established in 1980, this
privately funded institution offers over eighteen permanent
participatory installations. It also presents visual art exhibits
that show the connection between mathematics, science,
and art in, for example, the work of M.C. Escher or Salva-
dor Dali. The Experience Center is planning to move to the
Orange County Fairgrounds in late 1981, and it is advisable
to call for specific information when planning a visit.

JUNIOR ARTS CENTER

Barnsdall Park
4814 Hollywood Boulevard
Los Angeles, California 90027
(213) 666-1093
HOURS: Tuesday through Saturday 10 AM to 5 PM
During the school year, mornings are reserved for
school groups.
ADMISSION: Free
DIRECTIONS: Junction of Vermont Avenue and Holly-
    wood Boulevard. See Hollyhock House for informa-
    tion on directions, parking and public transportation.
WHEELCHAIR ACCESS: Yes

The Junior Arts Center is the epitome of a children's museum. It brilliantly blends exploration, participation, and
conceptual perception in one of the most exciting and innovative programs in the city.

Four or five major exhibitions each year present a
kaleidoscope of experiences that involve children and always, in some way, relate to fine art. Young people are
encouraged to discover new ideas through their involve-
ment in the exhibits. Equally important, youngsters also
learn to look at and appreciate the objects on display.

A sampling of exhibits best describes what the Junior
Arts Center is all about. In "Skyfishing," children learned
about the history, construction, and cultural differences of
kites, and they were invited to make a kite of their own.
"Light Fantastic" focused on the science and aesthetics of
light and involved experiments with light patterns on water,
color light mixing, and the effects of primary light colors on
objects of similar or opposite hues. Several artists who work
with light, color, and reflection designed special installations.
"The Stamp Act of 1979" included a variety of stamps,
from branding irons and William S. Hart's stamped saddle
to handmade postage stamps, Chinese chops, cookie cut-
ters and original rubber stamps. Children, of course,
stamped out their own art. For "The Blimp Show: Balloons,
Blimps and Dirigibles," the gallery was transformed into an
airship hangar and in "The Great American Foot Show,"
shoes, feet, and foot coverings were on display. "The
Printer's Proof" displayed prints by major artists (Rauschen-

berg, Oldenburg, and Ellsworth Kelly), and students could "pull a print" from a press installed nearby. Finally, "Mummies and Star Wars" featured a visual comparison between Egyptian and aerospace images in a tomb and space-capsule environment.

The Junior Arts Center is a magical place for children, but you don't have to be one to get in!

KIDSPACE

Rosemont Pavillion
700 Seco Street
Pasadena, California 91103
(213) 449-9143
HOURS: Kidspace is open March through July. From March through May, school groups are scheduled in the morning, and the general public is invited Monday through Friday from 3 to 5 PM and on Saturday from 9:30 AM to 12:30 PM. In June and July, Kidspace is open to the public Monday through Saturday from 9:30 AM to 5:30 PM
ADMISSION: Free
DIRECTIONS: From the Ventura Freeway, exit at Holly Street or Orange Grove and follow the signs to the Rose Bowl. From the 210, exit at Seco Street. Kidspace is one-quarter mile from the Rose Bowl.
PARKING: Lot.
WHEELCHAIR ACCESS: Yes

Don't be surprised if you experience the ghostly fragrance of wilted roses at Kidspace. This children's learning and exploring center is housed in the Rosemont Pavilion, a cavernous cement structure also used to build floats for the famed Tournament of Roses Parade.

Kidspace, established in 1980 by Pasadena's Junior League, presents a number of participatory exhibits geared to young people four to fourteen years of age. Although specific exhibits will change each year when the space reopens (it operates from March through July), general themes include visual arts; exploring different occupations; communications (kids can participate in a simulated TV studio); space and technology; measuring; and computers. Volunteers are available at each station to offer assistance and guidance, and each Saturday, free arts and crafts classes are offered to visitors. A gift shop on wheels roves throughout Kidspace selling inexpensive items that relate to specific exhibits.

LA HABRA CHILDREN'S MUSEUM

301 South Euclid Street
La Habra, California 90631
(714) 526-2229 Extension 271
(213) 694-1011
HOURS: Tuesday through Saturday, 10 AM to 4 PM
ADMISSION: $1.00 for adults; 50¢ for children.
DIRECTIONS: The museum is located in Portola Park between La Habra Boulevard and Lambert Road. From the Orange Freeway (57), exit at Lambert and turn onto Euclid (right if you were going south or left if coming from the north); from the Santa Ana Freeway (5), exit at Euclid and continue north; from the Pomona Freeway (60), take the Hacienda off ramp, turn east on Whittier Boulevard and then south of Euclid.
PARKING: Lot
PUBLIC TRANSPORTATION: RTD Line 820 (L.A.-Whittier-Brea) on La Habra Boulevard at Euclid Avenue
WHEELCHAIR ACCESS: Parts of the museum cannot be reached. No restrooms.
SHOP: A gift shop sells items and books of interest to children.
TOURS: Tours must be scheduled for groups of ten or

more. Tours are conducted between 10 AM and 3 PM and last one hour. No tours on Saturdays.

What better place for a children's museum than a converted railroad station? Established in 1977, the museum is a special place in which children are invited to explore various facets of their world through cultural, historical, and scientific "hands-on" installations. It is recommended for children ages 12 and under.

The old Union Pacific railroad depot has been restored to its original condition, with the former waiting room as Gallery #1 and the baggage room as Gallery #2. Actual railroad cars permanently located on the tracks adjacent to the museum are also used, and the caboose offers a special display on the history of La Habra.

The permanent installations include the Nature Walk, the Live Bee Observatory, the Model Train Village, Railroad Cars, Space Place, and Grandma's Attic. Changing exhibitions have included "Discovery Two," which offered fifty hands-on science projects demonstrating optical illusions, magnetism, electricity, light, sound, and gravity; and "Growing Things," which featured an investigation of seeds, soils, roots, herbs, and other related topics. "Fibers and Textiles" featured a display of the steps from raw fibers to finished products, demonstrations of weaving and spinning, and textile hangings; "Signs and Symbols" was an exhibit of city street signs, international signs, flags, and totem poles.

THE LOS ANGELES CHILDREN'S MUSEUM

310 North Main Street
Los Angeles, California 90012
(213) 687-8800
HOURS: Weekdays subject to change depending on the
    season; call for specific information. The museum is
open to the general public on Saturday and Sunday from 10 AM to 4:30 PM. School and community groups of ten or more must make advance reservations by calling (213) 687-8801.

ADMISSION: $2.50 for adults; $1.50 for children and senior citizens. Special groups rates are available.

DIRECTIONS: Atop the City Hall Mall at the corner of Temple and Main Streets, four blocks east of the Music Center. From the Harbor Freeway (which connects with the Santa Monica, Hollywood and Pasadena Freeways) take the Los Angeles Street off-ramp, exit right onto Los Angeles Street, and the museum is on the right. From the Santa Ana Freeway, exit at Alameda Street and turn left on Los Angeles Street.

PARKING: Limited street parking. Underground lot with validated parking below the museum at Los Angeles Street or a block away at Union Station (800 North Alameda).

PUBLIC TRANSPORTATION: RTD Lines 2 and 92-Main Street. All CBD routes to Minibus 202 on Los Angeles Street.

WHEELCHAIR ACCESS: The entire museum is accessible to the handicapped. People using wheelchairs can enter the museum on North Main Street or may come directly into the museum via the garage elevator. Several exhibits are designed specifically for handicapped children.

DINING: Restaurants and snack bars are available on the Mall Level. Bag lunches may be eaten on the grass in front of the museum.

SHOP: A selection of children's books, educational toys and games (many under $1.00), and craft items.

I hear and I forget
I see and I remember
I do and I understand—motto of The L.A. Children's Museum

In the Children's Museum, you will find neither stuffed children nor paintings hung at kid level. In fact, you won't see much that directly relates to art. What you will discover is an amazing place—modeled after the successful Boston Children's Museum—that offers an environment to enrich, excite, and delight children of all ages.

The museum is a "hands-on" learning laboratory based on the premise that children learn by doing. It provides a variety of experiences which integrate music, art, science, humanities, and technology. Filled with oversized and unusual things, and designed primarily for two- to fourteen-year-olds (although many fourteen-year-olds might find it a bit insulting), it encourages touching, exploring and handling. The Children's Museum is a place of magical discovery where no one fails and everyone learns, even if they don't quite realize it. The museum's cavernous space is divided into specific exhibits, each one supervised by interns who assist the visitors. The exhibition space includes the following:

City Streets: An exhibit in which children can walk, crawl, or climb while they see, hear, and feel "The City." Props of the city prompt children to enact city happenings and help a child integrate his or her understanding of how a city works.

Sticky City: A room filled with a great variety of oversized foam shapes that stick to each other and to the walls and ceilings. The construction possibilities are endless. This was designed by a developmental psychologist and has particular advantages for special-needs children.

The Shadow Box: Children step into this "magic space" to dance, jump, bend, and stretch—they step away and their shadows are "frozen" on walls of phosphorescent vinyl.

Zoetrope Room: Here children learn about the development of animated films. They can design their own animation strips to be viewed through a "zoetrope"—a primitive form of moving picture technology.

Investigations Underground: Descend beneath a manhole cover, crawl through a sewer pipe, and discover the complex system of pipes and wires hidden under the streets that keep a city in operation.

Newsroom: The newsroom exhibit is a small-scale working replica of a television newsroom. Children can participate in many aspects of TV news production in front of the camera (as an anchorperson or weather reporter) as well as behind the scenes (operating the camera or audio equipment).

How Would I Feel: Through miniature displays, real-life props, and equipment such as X-ray viewing boxes, stethoscopes, and braille typewriters, children experience what it would be like to be blind or deaf or to make a visit to the hospital.

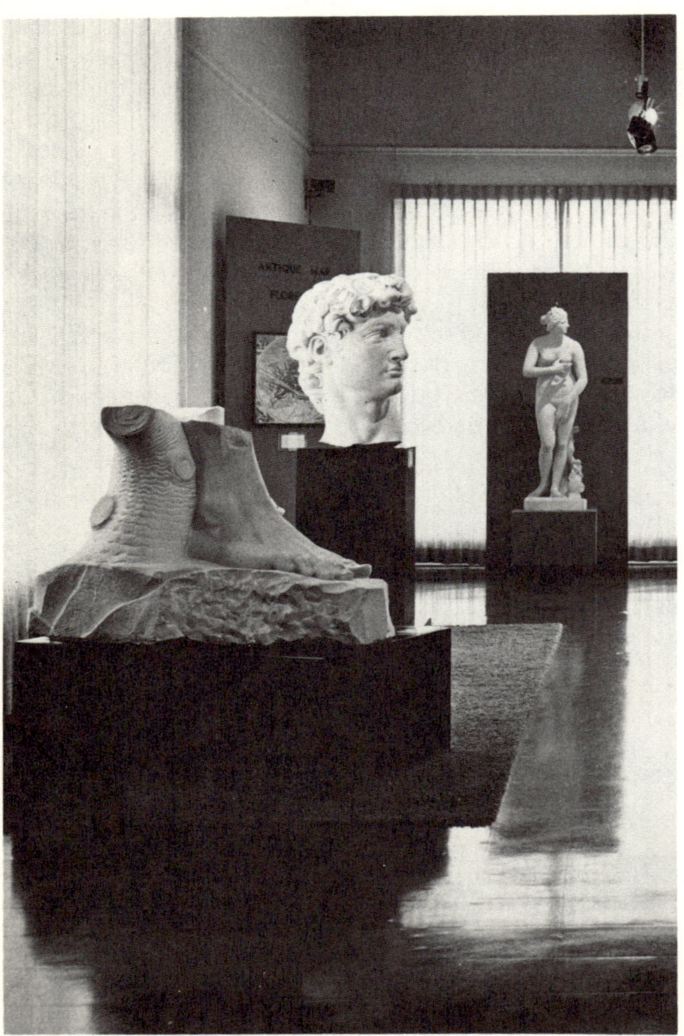

Forest Lawn Museum, Glendale

SPECIAL MUSEUMS

The museums in this section feature unusual or fascinating collections which defy categorization. Most of them are worth a visit if you happen to be in the neighborhood. Transportation museums (automobiles, trains, and planes), wax museums, and strictly commercial enterprises that call themselves museums have not been included. It is advisable to call and reconfirm hours and days of operation if you are planning a special trip.

Since these museums are small, most do not have dining facilities or special programs. Wheelchair accessibility, except in public institutions, is limited.

CALIFORNIA OIL MUSEUM

1003 East Main Street
Santa Paula, California 93060
(805) 525-6672
HOURS: Wednesday through Sunday, 10 AM to 4:30 PM
ADMISSION: Free
DIRECTIONS: At Tenth and Main Streets in downtown
    Santa Paula. From the Ventura Freeway (west), get on
    Highway 126 and exit at Tenth Street.

This small museum is dedicated to the oil industry in California in the 1800s. It features a collection of early oil-drilling equipment, documents, and photographs. Operated by Union Oil, the museum offers a unique audio tour complete with sound effects.

DUNBAR MUSEUM OF BLACK CULTURE AND HISTORY

4233 South Central Avenue
Los Angeles, California 90011
(213) 233-7168

HOURS: Monday through Friday, 9:30 AM to 4:30 PM.
ADMISSION: Free
DIRECTIONS: Harbor Freeway (south) to Santa Barbara
    exit; turn right on Central to 42nd Street.
PUBLIC TRANSPORTATION: RTD Line 3 (Central Ave-
    nue) at 42nd Street

The Dunbar Hotel, named for the black poet, was the first hotel in the United States built for and by blacks. Opened in 1928, the hotel and its Club Alabam became a haven for black entertainers such as Ella Fitzgerald, Count Basie, Lena Horne, Fats Waller, and Nat King Cole. Today, the hotel is designated an historical landmark, and the museum, founded by Bernard Johnson in 1976, is dedicated to presenting black culture and history. Mr. Johnson hopes to restore the hotel to its original condition and plans to dedicate each of the 115 hotel guest rooms to a different personality in black history. The museum is especially concerned with telling young black children about their cultural heritage.

WILLIAM S. HART RANCH AND MUSEUM

24151 Newhall Avenue
Newhall, California
(805) 259-0855
HOURS: Grounds open daily, 10 AM to sundown; museum
    open Wednesday through Friday from 10 AM to 3:30
    PM and on weekends from 10 AM to 5 PM.
ADMISSION: Free
DIRECTIONS: Interstate 5 to Interstate 14 (Palmdale-Lan-
    caster); exit at San Fernando Road and continue two
    miles.
PUBLIC TRANSPORTATION: Locally served by Grey-
    hound.

Cowboy film star William S. Hart (1865-1946) lived on this estate, which is now a 230-acre park operated by Los Angeles County. Hart's home, which is the museum, features a collection of western paintings and sculpture, including works by Charles Russell and Frederick Remington.

THE FOREST LAWN MUSEUM

Forest Lawn Memorial Park
1217 South Glendale Avenue
Glendale, California 91209
(213) 254-3131
HOURS: Daily, 10 AM to 6 PM
ADMISSION: Free
DIRECTIONS: Golden State Freeway (south) to the Los
    Feliz Boulevard off-ramp (east). Turn east on Los Feliz
    to Glendale Avenue, then turn right on Glendale to
    the main gate of Forest Lawn Memorial Park.
PARKING: Follow signs to the museum, where parking is
    available.
PUBLIC TRANSPORTATION: Line 56 (Los Angeles-Sun-
    land) on Glendale Avenue at Park entrance. Line 39
    (Los Angeles-Glendale-Burbank) and Line 436 (Holly-
    wood-Glendale-Pasadena) on Brand Boulevard at Los
    Feliz.
WHEELCHAIR ACCESS: Good
DINING: None (no picnics)
SHOP: The Memento Shop sells slides, china plates, souve-
    nirs from Forest Lawn, and booklets on various attrac-
    tions within the park. It has a rather good selection of
    general books on Michelangelo.
FOCUS: Reproductions of famous sculptures with a few
    original pieces of art.

The Forest Lawn Museum overlooks acres of graves but does not, as one might imagine, present the history of embalming or even a survey of tombstone styles. The museum has a small selection of original art works, and the memorial park features reproductions of art masterpieces. Dr. Hubert Eaton, the founder of Forest Lawn, believed sculpture was nicer than mismatched mausoleums, and he thought a cemetery should be a place for the living and not just a repository for the dead.

The museum houses Dr. Eaton's collection of original bronzes, including works by Frederic Remington, J. Clinton Shepard, Charles Russell, Gutzon Borglum (he was responsible for Mount Rushmore), Jose Belloni, and Jesse Beasley. Ancient coins mentioned in the Bible, a suit of armor, gemstones, and some miniature portraits are also on display.

However, the most fascinating, if not bizarre, aspect of the museum collection is its "serious reproductions," which include a plaster of Paris reproduction of Ghiberti's *Paradise Doors* made from molds taken from the original bronze doors in Florence, Italy. Another reproduction is "The Sotterraneo," the room beneath the Medici Chapel in Florence covered with charcoal drawings by Michelangelo. Forest Lawn's reproduction of the thirty-three-by-nine-foot cell has been created with full-size photographic murals which, according to Forest Lawn, were made with the cooperation of the director of the Medici Chapel, Dr. Paolo dal Poggeto, who discovered the room in 1975.

Historians believe the artist hid in the tiny room for twelve weeks in 1530 in a successful effort to escape a political purge. Admission to the original Sotterraneo in Florence is restricted because of the small space and risk of damage to the drawings, and in some ways, Forest Lawn is not wrong in saying that their "Sotterraneo" is a unique opportunity to "see the only reproduction in the world of the Master's creative struggles."

But do not think the reproductions end here. As you enter the Forest Lawn Museum, you will be greeted by a colossal marble head. Could it be? Yes, it is the decapitated head of Michelangelo's *David*. During a recent earthquake, the sculpture fell, causing the young hero to lose his head. A new "David" now stands guard outside in the Court of David, but this other head gives the viewer a unique opportunity to marvel at the size of David's nostrils, an experience not possible while viewing the original in Italy.

The Memorial Park also boasts three original art works: *The Last Supper Window*, a remarkable re-creation of Leonardo da Vinci's masterpiece in stained glass; *The Crucifixion*, which is billed as America's largest religious painting, measuring 195 feet long and 45 feet wide; and *The Resurrection*, an original work commissioned for Forest Lawn that is presented throughout the day in a sound-and-light show.

Reproductions of the *Pieta*, *Moses*, and several other sculptures by Michelangelo, located in the Memorial Court of Honor, are reproduced in Carrara marble taken from the same quarries as the originals.

While a visit to Forest Lawn may not qualify as a serious art experience, we should pause to remember that the ancient Romans made "exact copies" of their most prized Greek statuary, and many of these Roman copies are in major museums today.

Forest Lawn also has numerous chapels and churches, all copies, and paying a visit to the memorial park is something everyone should do once in a lifetime.

HAWKINS DOLL MUSEUM

1437 Sixth Street
Santa Monica, California 90403
(213) 394-2981
HOURS: Friday, 1–5 PM; tours every hour
ADMISSION: $2.50 for adults; $1.50 for children.

DIRECTIONS: From the Santa Monica Freeway (west), exit
at Fifth Street. The museum is located between Santa
Monica Boulevard and Broadway.

This very small museum has over 3,500 dolls that range in
date from the 1500s to the mid-1950s. Collected by Beulah
Hawkins and her son, the dolls represent many different
countries and are randomly displayed in the Hawkins family
home, an 1890s Santa Monica classic. Mr. Hawkins, who
now operates this private museum, also buys, sells, and
repairs dolls.

THE REAL THING MUSEUM OF COCA–COLA MEMORABILIA

11650 Riverside Drive
North Hollywood, California 91602
(213) 980-3444
HOURS: Monday through Saturday, 11 AM to 4 PM
ADMISSION: Free
DIRECTIONS: Take the Ventura Freeway to the Laurel
Canyon exit, turn right, and continue four blocks to
Colfax Avenue. The museum is at Colfax and River-
side Drive.
PUBLIC TRANSPORTATION: RTD Line 20 (Magnolia) to
Colfax and Riverside. RTD Line 162 (Riverside-Glen-
dale) to Colfax.

This remarkable place has over three thousand items of
Coca–Cola advertising from 1891 to 1943, including special
displays of rare antiques, calendars, signs, toys, and games.
It was established in 1978 by Dr. Leonard Sidlow, a retired
orthodontist, and includes a store in which visitors can purchase less valuable Coca–Cola kitsch.

WILL ROGERS STATE HISTORIC PARK
(Western Art Collection)

14253 Sunset Boulevard
Pacific Palisades, California 90272
(213) 454-8212
HOURS: Daily, 10 AM to 5 PM
ADMISSION: $2.00 per vehicle; 50¢ for dogs.
DIRECTIONS: From the San Diego Freeway, take the Sun-
set Boulevard exit (west) past Brentwood to Will Ro-
gers State Park Road and turn right.
PUBLIC TRANSPORTATION: RTD Line 76

Will Rogers, the famous Hollywood cowboy who said ''I
never met a man I didn't like,'' lived on this 186-acre estate
beginning in 1928. He filled his thirty-one-room ranch house
with numerous examples of western art, including paintings
and sculptures by Charles Russell, Tex Wheeler, Charles
Beil, Howard Chandler Christy and Ed Borein. These
pieces, along with various Indian crafts from Cherokee,
Navajo, Toltec, Oaxaco, Blackfoot, and Sioux tribes, are
on display in the house, which is kept just as it was when
Rogers was alive. The ranch became a state park in 1944,
and includes hiking trails, a polo field, and stables.

SIMON WIESENTHAL CENTER
HOLOCAUST MUSEUM

Yeshiva University of Los Angeles
9760 West Pico Boulevard
Los Angeles, California 90035
(213) 553-9036 or 553-4478
HOURS: Monday through Thursday, 10:30 AM to 4:30 PM;
Friday, 10:30 AM to 2:30 PM; Sunday, 11 AM to 4 PM
ADMISSION: Free

DIRECTIONS: Located at Pico and Roxbury Drive, just east of Century City. From the Santa Monica Freeway, exit at Overland Avenue, go north to Pico, and turn right.
PUBLIC TRANSPORTATION: RTD Line 91S (Hollywood Boulevard to Beverly Drive and Pico). Santa Monica Municipal Bus Line #7 (Pico Boulevard). Pico at Roxbury to RTD 26 (W. Pico) at Rampau to downtown.

The knowledge of how it happened is the best insurance against its recurrence.—Simon Wiesenthal, at the dedication of the Simon Wiesenthal Center for Holocaust Studies in 1979

The Holocaust Museum is part of the Simon Wiesenthal Center for Holocaust Studies, an institution named for the famous hunter of Nazi war criminals. It is a museum of nightmares, dedicated to the hope that ''society will never allow an atrocity of the magnitude of the Holocaust to happen again.''

Affiliated with Yeshiva University of Los Angeles, the museum's primary goal is education. A variety of audio-visual techniques, graphics, photomurals, and other media convey the story of Nazi Germany. The sophisticated permanent installations include a special telephone hook-up in which visitors can monitor the public statements of world leaders during the Holocaust years of 1933 to 1945. It also features a mechanized information center that provides answers to the questions most often raised about this period of history.

One exhibit consists of multiple video monitors presenting recent news stories that deal with the denial of human rights. Datelines include Lebanon, Iran, Uganda, and other world locations where the center believes personal freedom is threatened.

The center sponsors classes, lectures, and a public outreach program.

GENERAL, NATURAL HISTORY, AND SCIENCE MUSEUMS

These museums do not concentrate on visual art, but they are important members of the museum community. Those which are concerned with cultural history and anthropology will often present art exhibits. Since most of these museums are public institutions, wheelchair access is adequate.

CALIFORNIA MUSEUM OF SCIENCE AND INDUSTRY

700 State Drive
Exposition Park
Los Angeles, California 90037
(213) 749-0101
HOURS: Daily, 10 AM to 5 PM
ADMISSION: Free
DIRECTIONS: From the Harbor Freeway (south), exit at Exposition Boulevard.
PUBLIC TRANSPORTATION: RTD Lines 5 and 6 on Santa Barbara
RTD Line 49 on Figueroa
RTD Line 41 (Alvarado) on Figueroa
RTD Line 18 on Exposition Boulevard
RTD Line 95 on Vermont

This is a science-and-technology educational center with twenty halls of permanent exhibits on health, natural resources, contemporary sciences, and industry. Sixty changing exhibits each year cover a broad spectrum of topics, including photography, sculpture, and an annual bonsai show.

EASTERN CALIFORNIA MUSEUM

155 Grant Street
Independence, California 93526

(714) 878-2411, extension 361.
HOURS: Sunday through Friday, 9 AM to 5 PM
ADMISSION: Free
DIRECTIONS: Independence is located in Inyo County.
    From Highway 396, exit at Center Street.

Located in the high desert, this county-owned general museum features Native American and pioneer artifacts, photographs, and documents, and natural history displays. The most interesting aspect of the museum is Little Pine Village, a group of restored buildings that include a general store, millinery shop, livery stable, blacksmith shop, and barber/beauty shop. Each building contains original objects that relate to the activities it involved. The museum's permanent collection also includes Paiute and Shoshone Indian baskets, beadwork, featherwork, and memorabilia relating to early mining, railroads, farming, and ranching.

LOS ANGELES COUNTY MUSEUM OF NATURAL HISTORY

900 Exposition Boulevard
Exposition Park
Los Angeles, California 90007
(213) 744-3438
HOURS: Tuesday through Sunday, 10 AM to 5 PM; second
    Tuesday of each month is a free day from noon to 9 PM
ADMISSION: $1.00 for adults, 50¢ for students, senior citizens, and children
PUBLIC TRANSPORTATION AND DIRECTIONS: See
    California Museum of Science and Industry.

In the grand tradition of a large natural history museum, this institution features extensive permanent exhibitions relating to earth sciences, history, and life science. Seemingly endless halls and corridors display insects, birds, shells, marine life, and cultural history from places such as the South Pacific, West Africa, and Australia. The museum includes a remarkable and beautifully installed collection of gems and minerals, classic cars from 1900 to 1930, and taxidermized animals in diorama settings (a favorite with children). In addition to its exhibitions, the museum is concerned with expeditions, laboratory research, study and research collections, and the conservation and preservation of objects and specimens.

The museum's Ethnic Art Shop has a fine selection of arts and crafts from around the world, and the Book Shop features a good inventory of books relating to areas represented in the museum. There is a cafeteria on the ground floor.

GEORGE C. PAGE MUSEUM OF LA BREA DISCOVERIES

5801 Wilshire Boulevard
Los Angeles, California 90036
(213) 936-2230 Information
(213) 933-7451 Administration
HOURS: Tuesday through Sunday, 10 AM to 5 PM; second
    Tuesday of each month, noon to 9 PM
ADMMISSION: $1.00 general admission, 50¢ for students, senior citizens and children. Second Tuesday of each month is free.
DIRECTIONS: On Wilshire Boulevard between Ogden Drive and Curson Avenue, adjacent to the Los Angeles County Museum of Art in Hancock Park.
PUBLIC TRANSPORTATION: RTD Line 89 running north and south on Fairfax Avenue and RTD Line 83 running east and west on Wilshire Boulevard.

"Discoveries at La Brea," a new satellite of the Los Angeles County Museum of Natural History, presents permanent exhibits that focus on Ice Age animals recovered from the La Brea Tar Pits. It features reconstructed skeletons of prehistoric animals, including California sabertooth cats, American mastodons, giant birds, and a twelve-foot-high Imperial Mammoth that weighed fifteen to twenty thousand pounds. A unique observation laboratory allows visitors to watch scientists work on fossil bones found in the La Brea excavations. Continuous films and multi-media presentations explain various facets of prehistory.

MUSEUM OF NORTH ORANGE COUNTY

301 North Pomona Avenue
Fullerton, California 92632
(714) 738-6545
HOURS: Tuesday through Friday, 10 AM to 3 PM; Saturday, 10 AM to 5 PM; Sunday; noon to 5 PM
ADMISSION: Free
DIRECTIONS: Take the Santa Ana Freeway to the Harbor Boulevard exit. Pomona Avenue is between Commonwealth Avenue and Chapman Boulevard.
PUBLIC TRANSPORTATION: RTD Line 800 (Los Angeles-Santa Ana) or RTD Line 846 (Artesia Boulevard) to Fullerton Park 'n Ride Station. OCTD #25 or #35.

The museum of North Orange County presents temporary and changing exhibits on science, history, and culture. The three permanent collections include North American Indians, paleontology, and an exhibit on energy and resources. Art-related exhibits have featured printmaking, papermaking, photography, antique clocks, and textiles. In addition to showing the art, the museum generally presents information displays which explain the processes used to create the art.

The museum building is the former Fullerton Public Library and is a prime example of 1930s Spanish-style architecture.

RIVERSIDE MUNICIPAL MUSEUM

3720 Orange Street
Riverside, California 92501
(714) 787-7273
HOURS: Tuesday through Friday, 9 AM to 5 PM; Saturday and Sunday, 1 to 5 PM
ADMISSION: Free
DIRECTIONS: Located at Seventh and Orange in downtown Riverside. From Highway 91 south, exit at Seventh Street; going north, exit at University Avenue and turn west on Seventh Street.
PUBLIC TRANSPORTATION: RTD Line 496 (Los Angeles-Riverside-San Bernardino), RTD Line 860 (Long Beach-Disneyland-Riverside) to RTD station at Seventh and Market—walk a short distance.

This general museum emphasizes local history, natural history, and prehistory. It is housed in the former Riverside Post Office (circa 1912)—a nice building with brass and marble interiors—and has an extremely fine collection of American Indian baskets from Southern California. Also see the listing under Heritage House.

SAN BERNARDINO MUSEUM

2024 Orange Tree Lane
Redlands, California 92373
(714) 792-1334
HOURS: Tuesday through Saturday, 9 AM to 5 PM; Sunday, 1 to 5 PM
ADMISSION: Free

DIRECTIONS: Just off Highway 10, between California and Alabama Streets

This is a general history museum that focuses on local history, prehistory, and natural history. Permanent displays feature fossils, rocks, minerals, and life mountings of birds, mammals, reptiles, and insects. Monthly art exhibits highlight work by local artists.

SAN DIEGO

The following three natural history and science museums are located in the El Prado section of Balboa Park. San Diego Transit Lines 7 or 7B serve all areas of the park.

SAN DIEGO MUSEUM OF MAN

(714) 239-2001
HOURS: Daily, 10:00 AM to 4:30 PM
ADMISSION: $1.00 for adults; 25¢ for children 6–16; free on Wednesday.

Permanent and rotating exhibitions feature ethnological and archeological material pertaining to peoples of the Americas. Textiles, archeology, and paleontology of the Southwest are the strongest collections in the museum.

SAN DIEGO MUSEUM OF NATURAL HISTORY

(714) 232-3821
HOURS: Daily 10 AM to 4:30 PM
ADMISSION: $1.00 for adults; children under 16 free. Tuesdays are free.

This regional history museum concentrates on Upper Baja California, Southern California, and regions of Arizona. It features birds, mammals, and botanical exhibits and has an especially active research department.

REUBEN H. FLEET SPACE THEATER AND SCIENCE CENTER

(714) 238-1168
HOURS: Monday through Friday, 10 AM to 5 PM and from 7–9:30 PM. Weekends from 9:30 AM to 10:30 PM.
ADMISSION: $1.00 for adults; 50¢ for children.

The Space Theater is an innovative planetarium which features changing shows, and the Science Center includes forty-five participatory or "hands-on" exhibits relating to science and technology. Permanent installations include optics of the eye, cloud chambers, and holography.

SANTA BARBARA MUSEUM OF NATURAL HISTORY

2559 Puesta del Sol Road
Santa Barbara, California 93105
(805) 682-4711
HOURS: Monday through Saturday, 9 AM to 5 PM; Sunday, 1 to 5 PM
ADMISSION: Free
DIRECTIONS: Take Highway 101 to Santa Barbara Street exit; turn right on Los Olivos and continue past the mission.
PUBLIC TRANSPORTATION: Local Santa Barbara bus transit lines may be picked up from the bus terminal at Chapala Street. A shuttle bus, picked up along State Street, goes directly to the museum.

This privately funded museum focuses on natural history and anthropology of the Pacific Coast, with an emphasis on the greater Santa Barbara region. Its strongest collections relate to ornithology and California Indian life. A small gallery features local art and photography. Each June the museum schedules a show of contemporary Indian art, and a performing arts festival is presented during the first week of October.

VENTURA COUNTY HISTORICAL MUSEUM

100 East Main Street
Ventura, California 93110
(805) 653-0323
HOURS: Tuesday through Sunday, 10 AM to 5 PM
ADMISSION: Free
DIRECTIONS: Take the Ventura Freeway to the California
    Street exit and turn left on Main Street.

This is a local history museum with permanent installations of Native American, Spanish, and pioneer artifacts. Temporary exhibits include five art exhibits: a county-wide competition and four one-artist shows based on the competition. During the summer, the museum features pieces from the George Stuart historical figure collection: fasincating one-quarter-of-life-size figures dressed in detailed costumes. The museum also has an extensive collection of historical California farm implements.

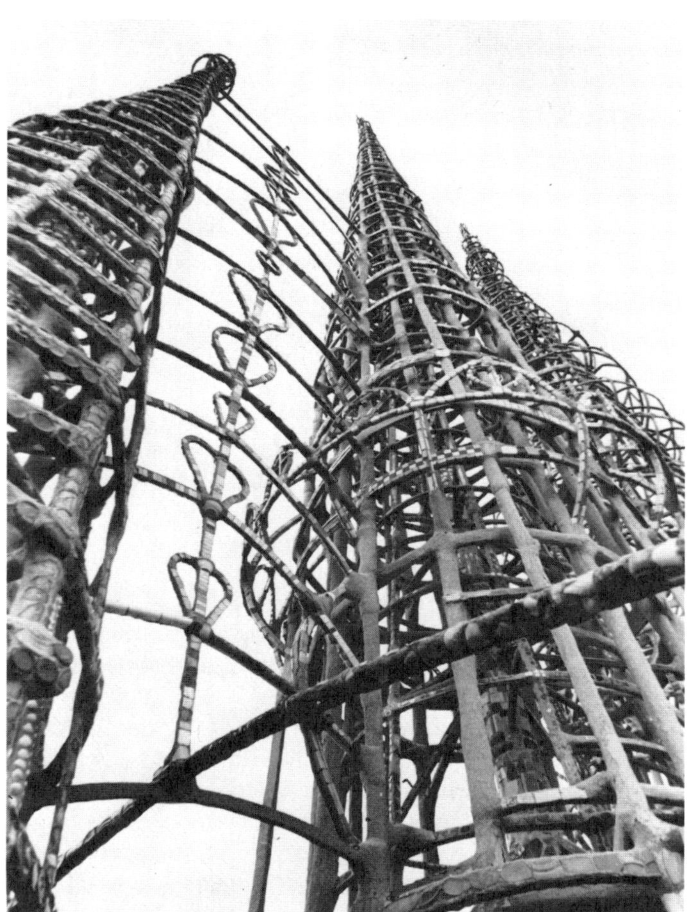

Watts Tower, Los Angeles

Community galleries and art center galleries are called "alternative spaces" because they fill the void between museums and commercial galleries. Purely and simply, they exhibit art and support the process of artistic creation. These galleries function as museums without permanent collections, since they feature changing exhibitions, and they operate in a manner similar to commercial galleries but without a sales or profit motive.

Most museums, even those that specialize in contemporary art, are reticent about displaying controversial ideas, experimental concepts, and unknown artists. Because of their financial concerns, commercial galleries will not take the risk of presenting unproven, unestablished artists whose work may not sell or may not be marketable in content.

Many artists, therefore, first exhibit at nonprofit galleries where, in many cases, the screening process is quite rigid and the requirements are high. Then they are represented by a small commercial gallery that specializes in new artists, move on to a big "name" gallery, and eventually appear in a museum exhibition.

The main difference between community art galleries and art centers is that the art centers have a more general, less experimental exhibition philosophy and are extensions of a city department.

The community galleries each have a very specific point of view, are more directed toward the art community, and rely on membership support, government grants, and corporate donations.

Although all of these galleries have nonprofit status, the art on display is often for sale. In most cases, the galleries act only as a liaison between the artist and the buyer. If a commission is involved, it is a small fraction of the sale price, unlike the 40 percent averaged by most commercial galleries.

With rare exception, nonprofit galleries do not have dining facilities or book shops. If an institution provides either of these services or offers specific education programs, that information is included in the general overview.

COMMUNITY GALLERIES

ARCO CENTER FOR VISUAL ART

Atlantic Richfield Plaza
505 South Flower Street
Los Angeles, California 90071
(213) 488-0038
HOURS: Monday through Friday, 10 AM to 6 PM; Saturday, 11 AM to 5 PM
ADMISSION: Free
DIRECTIONS: The ARCO Plaza is at Fifth and Flower Streets in downtown Los Angeles. From the Harbor Freeway, exit at Sixth Street and turn left on Flower.
PARKING: Validated parking is available during the week at 400 South Flower Street (across from the ARCO Plaza) and on Saturdays in the ARCO Tower parking facility at Fifth and Flower Streets.
PUBLIC TRANSPORTATION: Most downtown RTD lines, including 820, 49, 757, and 758.
WHEELCHAIR ACCESS: Good. Elevators from the Plaza garage to B Level.
FOCUS: Changing exhibits of contemporary art.

The ARCO Center for Visual Art organizes exhibitions of contemporary art in all mediums, including painting, sculpture, photography, prints, drawings, and design, with an emphasis on West Coast artists.

The center, which opened in 1976, is funded, but not directly controlled, by the Atlantic Richfield Oil Corporation, and presents fourteen exhibits each year. It has a large exhibition area for paintings, sculpture, and other large-scale works, plus a smaller gallery for photography and prints. Although most of the art on display is available for sale, the center takes no commissions from sales, but will act as a liaison between the artist and the purchaser.

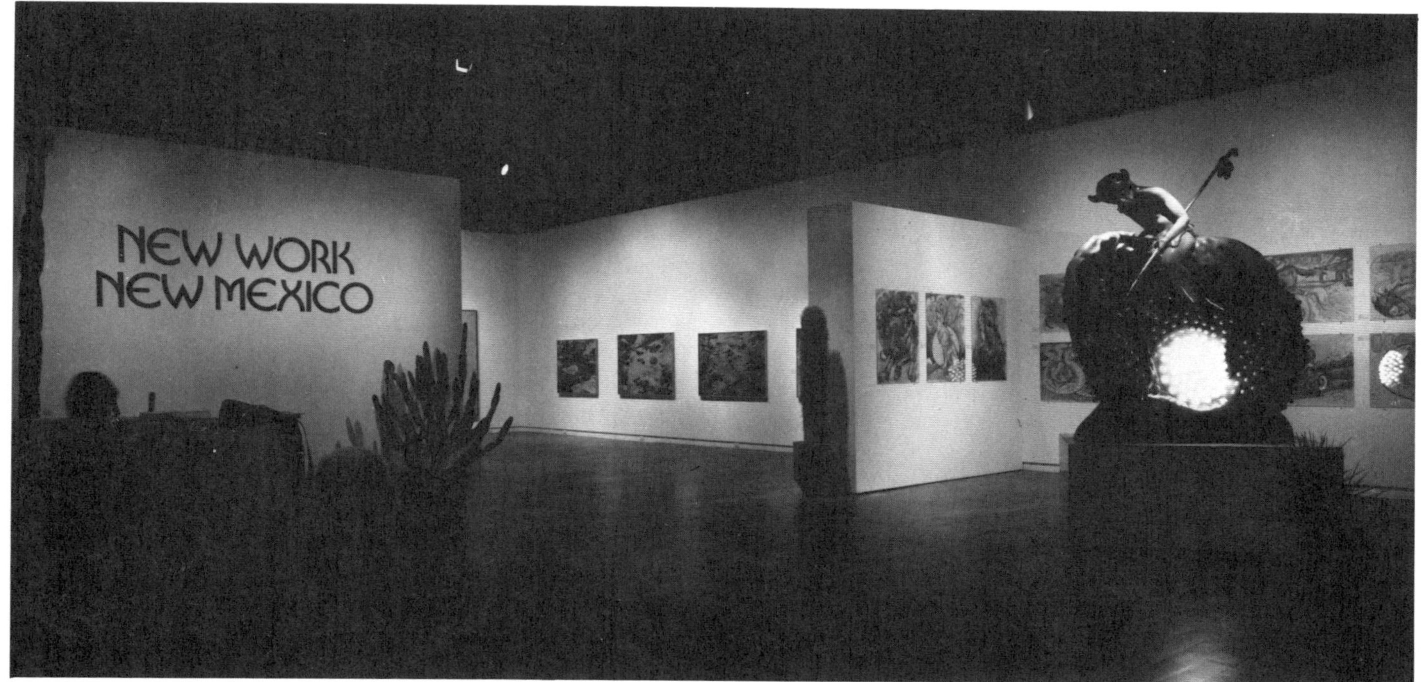

ARCO Center for Visual Art, L.A.

New ideas and consistent artistic development and execution are the major criteria for the exhibits that the ARCO Center organizes. Consideration is also given to new artists who are not well established or whose work is not commercial. Although the center does not offer formal education programs, its choice of exhibitions demonstrates a concern for making contemporary art accessible to general audiences. It offers a broad overview of the contemporary art scene by presenting a balance of experimental shows and shows that are more traditional. Exhibits have included the work of Austrian artist Herbert Bayer, the last living Bauhaus artist (an exhibit that traveled to the Museum of Modern Art in New York); a light-illusion space built into the gallery by Jim Turrell (especially significant because most institutions cannot afford to make this type of installation); and "Downtown Los Angeles Under Water," a mural proposal by Los Angeles street-mural master Terry Schoonhoven. Two exhibits, "American Indian Art" and "Fantasy Clothes/Fantastic Costumes," demonstrate that the center is not locked into any one direction. "Photographer's Photographers" illustrated the center's unique approach to discovering contemporary artists. In this exhibit, four well-known photographers were asked to select four people whose work they thought should be exhibited.

The result: the work of twelve very different, very exciting photographers.

CAMERAVISION

Los Altos Building
4121 Wilshire Boulevard
Los Angeles, California 90010
(213) 380-4266
HOURS: Wednesday through Sunday, Noon to 5 PM;
    Thursday, 7:30 to 10:30 PM
ADMISSION: Free
DIRECTIONS: Between Crenshaw and Western Boulevard. From the Santa Monica Freeway, exit at Crenshaw and drive north.
PARKING: Street only
PUBLIC TRANSPORTATION: RTD Line 83
WHEELCHAIR ACCESS: No
FOCUS: Changing exhibits of contemporary photography.

We support those photographers exploring new areas of expression and offer encouragement, criticism, technical information and exhibition experiences to all photographers.—Cameravision brochure

Cameravision, which evolved from a commercial gallery, is a nonprofit cooperative gallery for photographers who have not yet exhibited in museums or commercial galleries.

Prospective members must submit a portfolio that is reviewed by a special selection committee. Photographers who are accepted then have an opportunity to exhibit in the Cameravision gallery; thus, Cameravision functions more as a cooperative than as a gallery.

Perhaps one of the most important aspects of Cameravision is that it is a place where photographers and the general public can explore topics and exchange ideas. In one program, "Artist Hotseat," a photographer will present his or her work, discuss personal concerns and processes, and then conduct a question-and-answer period with the audience. "Exchange," which meets every Thurday at 7:30 PM, is an open forum in which photographers are encouraged to share their work and "explore their own aesthetic, artistic process, goals and motivation in an intense group exchange." Cameravision also presents lectures and provides workshops.

LOS ANGELES CENTER FOR PHOTOGRAPHIC STUDIES (LACPS)

814 South Spring Street, Third Floor
Los Angeles, California 90014
(213) 462-0578
HOURS: Tuesday through Saturday, 1 to 5 PM
ADMISSION: Free; ring buzzer to be admitted.
DIRECTIONS: From the Harbor Freeway, exit at Ninth Street. LACPS is between Eighth and Ninth Streets.
PARKING: Pay lots only.
PUBLIC TRANSPORTATION: RTD Lines 7, 8, 75, and 625 run along Spring Street, while Lines 755, 28, and 9 go up Eighth Street.
WHEELCHAIR ACCESS: Yes; use elevator.
FOCUS: Contemporary photography.

The Los Angeles Center for Photographic Studies (LACPS) is working to establish photography as an important force in the visual art community by stimulating and encouraging the reception of photography as a fine art.

The center, which was established in 1973 and recently opened its present gallery space, sponsors exhibits, lectures, and publications. It has also organized major exhibits for other institutions. LACPS has a broad-based membership of serious photographers and collectors, with a number of important West Coast artists serving on the board of trustees. It has published two major portfolios—*Silver See* in 1977 and *LA. Issue* in 1979—which featured the work of West Coast photographers.

LOS ANGELES CONTEMPORARY EXHIBITIONS (LACE)

240 South Broadway
Third Floor
Los Angeles, California 90012
(213) 620-0104
HOURS: Tuesday through Saturday, 11 AM to 5 PM
ADMISSION: Free
DIRECTIONS: From the Harbor/Pasadena Freeway, take the Fourth Street exit (west). From the Hollywood Freeway, exit on Broadway (south). Located on Broadway between Second and Third Streets.
PARKING: Paid lots only. (Least expensive lots are located on Spring and Main Streets.)
PUBLIC TRANSPORTATION: RTD Lines 5, 6, 12, 26 or busway at Third.
WHEELCHAIR ACCESS: Good
FOCUS: Changing contemporary exhibits

The position of an unestablished artist is painful; there is both social and economic isolation. Many of these artists are exploring aesthetic frontiers and this tends to isolate them further from both the general community and the established art community . . . The nature of much contemporary art is highly explorative and raw; the alternative space can provide an appropriate forum for this work.—LACE publication

Los Angeles Contemporary Exhibitions (LACE) concentrates on supporting experimental art not generally shown in museums or commercial galleries. Concerned with bringing serious new works to public attention, it is one indication of the emergence of downtown Los Angeles as an art center, and it recognizes the many artists now living and working in the area.

The open gallery spaces in this old office building offer a formal yet friendly space in which to view art. On the way to LACE, visitors have an opportunity to view a "bridal diorama"—one of those marvelous archaic window displays featuring a complete bridal party, including a plaster-of-paris cake, eternally frozen. One wonders if LACE selected its name because the acronym suited the location. Established in 1977, LACE is staffed entirely by artists and receives its financial support from government and foundation grants and memberships and fund-raising events, as well as corporate and individual contributions.

Each year, LACE sponsors twelve major exhibitions which include solo, group, and thematic shows which, according to the organization's literature, "show a wide spectrum of work, from the representational to the conceptual, from easily understood and accessible art to difficult and esoteric expressions."

Organized by LACE staff and guest curators, the exhibits range from video and audio pieces and installation pieces to sculpture, drawings, and paintings. Recent exhibits include "Testimonios de Latinoamerica," a group show of over a hundred works that presented political art from Latin American countries; "The Animal Show," which featured paintings and sculpture by seven artists using animals as central thematic material; "23 Days, 5 Installations," which featured installation pieces created specifically for the gallery space; and "Public Spirit," the first major performance festival in the Los Angeles area that focused on performance and other non-static work by Los Angeles artists.

One-person shows have featured Judy Pfaff, David Schirm, and Craig Antrium. LACE states: "The range of experience is large, with some artists having exhibited at the Whitney Museum, the Museum of Modern Art, Hirschhorn Museum and having major gallery affiliations. Other artists are newcomers, recently graduated or recently making public work produced in the isolation of the studio.''

There is also a strong emphasis on performance events, which usually are presented in the evening.

Although LACE speaks primarily to the art community, it has demonstrated a remarkable interest in reaching the general public. It has sponsored the work of older artists and conducted a series of art workshops in senior centers, a program supported by the National Endowment for the Arts. LACE artists also have taught and lectured in public schools, and from 1977 to 1979, LACE encouraged mural painting and provided demonstrations on mural techniques. Each year, LACE sponsors a Downtown Show which features the work of local artists, and it has an Open Studio Tour which highlights artists' studios in downtown Los Angeles.

LOS ANGELES ART ASSOCIATION GALLERIES

825 North La Cienega Boulevard
Los Angeles, California 90069
(213) 652-8272
HOURS: Tuesday through Friday, noon to 5 PM; Saturday, noon to 4 PM; Sunday, 2 to 4 PM
ADMISSION: Free
DIRECTIONS: On La Cienega's ''gallery row,'' between Melrose and Santa Monica. From the Santa Monica Freeway, exit at La Cienega (north).
PARKING: Street parking
WHEELCHAIR ACCESS: Yes
PUBLIC TRANSPORTATION: RTD Line 27
FOCUS: Exhibits featuring members' work.

The Los Angeles Art Association Galleries' prime location in the heart of ''gallery row'' and its credible name are slightly misleading. This is a nonprofit, self-supporting gallery which exhibits the work of its five hundred artist-members. It features monthly exhibits of artists who tend to do mainstream, traditional work. Established in 1924, the gallery does screen its members (applicants must submit three examples of their work), but the art seems somewhat pedestrian. (There are, of course, exceptions.) The gallery sells what is on exhibit and takes only a small commission. Exhibits tend to be group shows with a central theme such as ''Fantasy and Allegory,'' ''Animal World,'' or ''The World in Lines.'' Each month, the gallery sponsors a Sunday afternoon lecture that relates to the current exhibition. (Science-fiction author Ray Bradbury spoke in conjunction with the ''Fantasy and Allegory'' exhibit.)

LOS ANGELES INSTITUTE OF CONTEMPORARY ART

2020 South Robertson Boulevard
Los Angeles, California 90034
(213) 559-5033
HOURS: Tuesday through Saturday, noon to 6 PM
ADMISSION: Free
DIRECTIONS: On Robertson Boulevard near Cadillac Avenue; south of Pico Boulevard. From the Santa Monica Freeway, exit at Robertson Boulevard and go north.
PARKING: Street only
PUBLIC TRANSPORTATION: RTD Line 877 (Hollywood-Robertson Boulevard-Culver City). Robertson at Cadillac.
WHEELCHAIR ACCESS: Yes
FOCUS: Changing exhibits of experimental art, performance, and video art.

LAICA is an arena where ideas, issues and artistic needs of artists are given highest priority.—LAICA publication

The Los Angeles Institute of Contemporary Art (LAICA) primarily presents the work of experimental, innovative, and unconventional artists who probably would not have the opportunity, or the desire, to exhibit in traditional institutions. Some say this alternative space presents the "cutting edge" of contemporary art in Southern California. Others describe it as the "elite of the avant-garde."

Established in 1974, the institute is concerned with the needs and interests of the Los Angeles art community—albeit a relatively select segment of the art population, since LAICA is not interested in traditional or figurative art. According to its founder and director, Robert Smith, LAICA presents ideas and concepts that are (1) too new and experimental for museums; (2) too uncommercial to sell in galleries; and (3) too controversial, if not offensive, for establishment institutions—such as the performance artist who concludes each performance by cutting herself with a razorblade. Consideration is also given to artists who have not had an opportunity to exhibit their work.

Each year, LAICA's Exhibition Committee selects nine or ten major and fifteen minor exhibitions submitted by prospective curators. When a proposal is selected, the curator is given unrestricted control and assumes responsibility for the resulting exhibition. Exhibitions range from group shows of over three hundred artists to those featuring single artists.

Although LAICA directs most of its energies toward local artists, a portion of the exhibits feature national and international artists. LAICA rarely features "name" artists, because either they no longer need LAICA or their work is no longer new. Art emphasizing social or political messages constitutes a small portion of the exhibition calendar.

Representative exhibits include "Tableau," in which fifteen different artists were given an equal amount of space in the gallery to create theatrically oriented installations; "Unstretched Surfaces," which featured six artists from France and six from Southern California who paint on unstretched canvas (this was in conjunction with the Georges Pompidou Center in Paris); "Sound," presenting artists who create sound sculptures and make musical instruments; and "Polar Crossing," offering performance works by three European artists. In addition to its exhibits, LAICA offers an extensive variety of performance events (two to four each month) and a full schedule of video exhibitions and events.

LAICA makes no real effort to educate the public about the art it presents—art which is often difficult if not impossible to comprehend; nor does it encourage the uninitiated to participate. This exclusion of the general public is quite intentional. LAICA sees itself as an alternative to museums and commercial galleries, and basically exists for the art community.

The installation spaces at LAICA are well suited for the type of art presented, although the atmosphere is not particularly warm or inviting. LAICA has become the barometer of experimental artistic expression in Los Angeles and has expanded its efforts to two new locations: a ten-by-ten-foot window space in downtown Los Angeles—at Ninth between Hill and Broadway—that features special installations (this is the institute's one attempt to reach the public); and a satellite gallery at 815 Traction Avenue, downtown near little Tokyo, which generally presents performances and photography exhibits.

A quarterly *Journal*, published by LAICA 1974, includes articles, interviews, original art, and fiction. Guest editors determine theme and point of view. LAICA also has an artists' slide registry of over ten thousand slides of current work by more than fifteen hundred Southern California artists—the largest of its type in the United States.

MUNICIPAL ART GALLERY, LOS ANGELES

Barnsdall Park
4804 Hollywood Boulevard
Hollywood, California 90027
(213) 660-2200
HOURS: Tuesday through Sunday, 12:30 to 5 PM
ADMISSION: 50¢ for adults, children under 12 Free
DIRECTIONS: Located at Hollywood Boulevard and Vermont Avenue. See listing for Hollyhock House.
PARKING: In the park
PUBLIC TRANSPORTATION: See listing for Hollyhock House.
WHEELCHAIR ACCESS: Yes
FOCUS: Changing exhibits of contemporary art.

An important goal is to see contemporary art as the reflection of contemporary life, thoughts and events. If the visual language is different from that of Rembrandt, we need to teach people that language—or at least translate—so their fears are eliminated.—Josine Ianco-Starrels, Director, Municipal Art Gallery

The Municipal Art Gallery (MUNI) is a dynamic institution which showcases contemporary Southern California artists in a series of constantly changing exhibitions. It is distinguished by a strong commitment to bridge the gap between the art community and the general public.

The gallery, which is operated by the Los Angeles Municipal Arts Commission, presents sixteen exhibits each year and usually features two separate shows at any given time. All of the exhibits are designed, organized, and installed by the gallery, which has earned a well-deserved reputation for presenting important and innovative shows. According to gallery director Josine Ianco-Starrels, the Municipal Art Gallery "has no allegiance to any special style" for its exhibitions and "is pledged to showing fine work representing the concerns of artists from all communities, regardless of (1) what's hot in New York, (2) what is saleable, or (3) what is accepted by the art establishment." She believes it is important to "end visual illiteracy" because "art may be meaningful and important to all who care to make the effort to learn this language."

Exhibits at MUNI fall into three major categories: retrospectives of major West Coast artists (Helen Lundeberg, Joyce Treiman, Matsumi Kanemitsu, Charles White, and Peter Alexander, among many); shows that present the immediate concerns and interests of the art community (xerography, portraits); and theme or idea shows that focus on an aspect of the creative process. This latter category is an educational vehicle directed at the general public but usually well received by the art community. Past exhibits, which tend to be mixed-media, have included "Abstractions/Sources/Transitions," which explored the creative process; "Artists as Social Critics;" "The Object Observed," in which artists selected objects, from shoes to Japanese screens, for display; "By Moonlight," which focused on poetic works; and "In a Major and Minor Scale," which looked at how artists work with scale.

Each December, fantasy objects are featured in the "Magical Mystery Tour," an exhibit designed for children. Every two years, in the fall, MUNI mounts the "Newcomers Show," which showcases the work of fifteen unknown artists.

Most of the exhibits include statements by the artists in which they describe thought processes, technical information, or anything that might illuminate what their artwork is all about. Additionally, each Saturday at noon when an exhibit is running, the gallery offers "Conversations with the Artists," in which artists represented in the exhibit talk informally about their work. The gallery's interest in communicating about art is reflected in its innovative education program, developed by museum educator Nancy Walch, which features group discussions conducted by specially trained gallery guides. These special dialogues are offered at 2 PM Tuesday through Sunday. When you conclude one of these tours, you will not only have a better understanding of the art of display, but will have received insight about viewing and experiencing art in general.

If you happen to visit on a day when an exhibit is being installed, you will be welcome to explore how a show is mounted—a behind-the-scenes look not generally afforded to visitors either for security reasons or because of logistics. Such an opportunity helps us to appreciate that exhibits take a great deal of hard work and do not magically appear on gallery walls.

SECURITY PACIFIC PLAZA GALLERY

Security Pacific Plaza
333 South Hope Street
Los Angeles, California 90051
HOURS: Daily, 10 AM to 4 PM
ADMISSION: Free
DIRECTIONIS: The Security Pacific Building, a 55-story monolith, is located at the corner of Hope and Flower Streets in downtown Los Angeles. Use the Fourth Street exit of the Harbor Freeway.
PARKING: Parking is available under the Plaza, but the gallery does not validate parking certificates.
PUBLIC TRANSPORTATION: Minibus Line 202 to Hope and Flower.
WHEELCHAIR ACCESS: Yes
FOCUS: Changing exhibitions of contemporary art.

The rough granite walls, reflective granite floors, and expansive space of the Security Pacific Plaza create an interesting, often overwhelming, space in which to view contemporary art.

The gallery space, part of the Plaza's lobby, presents innovative exhibits of contemporary West Coast artists. The exhibits offer a unique opportunity for people who work in the building and for the general public to experience a wide range of visual arts.

Exhibits, which vary in length from six weeks to three months, have included ''Billy Al Bengston: Paintings of the 70s;'' ''Hang It On a Star,'' which featured costumes from movies; ''Contemporaries: 17 Artists,'' an important exhibit that showcased the work of major women artists from Los Angeles; ''Woods Davey Sculpture;'' ''West Coast Clay Spectrum,'' a group show of forty-eight artists' work; ''Photographic Directions;'' and ''On Fabric,'' an exhibit of fabric art by thirty-four artists and designers.

The gallery is part of a cultural program supported by the Security Pacific National Bank, an organization recognized for its extensive corporate art collection.

SENIOR EYE GALLERY

Palmcrest House
3501 Cedar Avenue
Long Beach, California 90807
(213) 595-4551
HOURS: Wednesday through Sunday, 2 PM to 4 PM
ADMISSION: Free
DIRECTIONS: Between Pacific Avenue and Long Beach Boulevard, easily reached from the San Diego Freeway at the Long Beach Boulevard exit or from the Long Beach Freeway at the Pacific Avenue exit.
PARKING: Lot at the Palmcrest House
PUBLIC TRANSPORTATION: RTD Lines 36, 423, or 841 to Long Beach Boulevard at Wardlow—about one-quarter mile walk to the gallery.
WHEELCHAIR ACCESS: Good
FOCUS: Changing contemporary exhibits

People become old when they do more and more for the last time and less and less for the first time.—Senior Eye Gallery

The Senior Eye Gallery is the first fine art gallery in the nation to be sponsored within a retirement center. Although the gallery is designed for senior citizens who live at Palmcrest House, it is open to the general public and presents excellent exhibits. The Senior Eye Gallery does not, as one might expect, feature sentimental paintings that society expects little old ladies to like. Instead, it exhibits the work of such major contemporary artists as Claire Falkenstein, Nicholas Brigante, Alice Asmar, Hans Burkhardt, and Gloria Kisch.

Dr. Julian Feingold, Director of Palmcrest House, says the Senior Eye Gallery ''reminds us that there exist interdependent physical, psychological, social, and aesthetic commitments that encourage the living of not only longer, but fuller lives.'' He adds that ''it is a broadening experience to witness the frail, in wheelchairs, or with walkers or canes, musing before the work of Claire Falkenstein.''

During the gallery's first five years of operation, over ninety thousand dollars' worth of artworks were sold. The gallery takes no commission, and all proceeds go to the artists, which makes the gallery beneficial not only to the elderly and the Long Beach community, but to artists as well.

WEST COLORADO GALLERY

108 West Colorado Boulevard
Pasadena, California
(213) 578-9461
HOURS: Tuesday through Saturday, 10 AM to 5 PM
DIRECTIONS: From Freeway 134 take the Colorado exit
    east for four blocks; galley is located just past the Norton Simon Museum.

This gallery, which was established by the Pasadena Community Arts Center in 1978, concentrates on exhibiting Southern California photographers in early or mid-career. Exhibits change every seven weeks and feature one artist.

WOMEN'S COMMUNITY GALLERIES

The Women's Building
1727 North Spring Street
Los Angeles, California 90012
(213) 221-6161
HOURS: Monday through Saturday, 10 AM to 5 PM
ADMISSION: Free
DIRECTIONS: From San Bernardino or Santa Monica Freeways, take the Alameda Street exit and continue
    north, parallel to the railroad tracks (away from downtown). Alameda turns into Spring Street. The Women's Building is on the edge of Chinatown.
PARKING: Street parking
PUBLIC TRANSPORTATION: No close stops
WHEELCHAIR ACCESS: None
FOCUS: Changing exhibitions of art by and relating to
    women.

The Women's Community Galleries in the Women's Building are alternative spaces for women that ''provide an historical and contemporary perspective of women, and honor the richness and diversity of women's experiences in a public environment.''

The Women's Building is an old three-story brick warehouse in a somewhat dismal industrial section of downtown Los Angeles. The Main Gallery, on the third level, features monthly exhibits that range from one-woman retrospectives to political/educational exhibits and juried shows which are selected by a special committee and coordinated in-house. Recent exhibits include "150 Contemporary Works on Paper by Women;" "Bedtime Stories: Women Speak Out About Incest;" and tapestries by Chilean women that represented social problems in Chile. "Women in American Architecture: An Historic and Contemporary Perspective" described the problems faced by women architects and examined the quality of their work; "Cross Pollination" featured a blending of traditional and contemporary art by Asian, Black, and Chicana women; and "By Mothers Show" presented work that explored the theme of motherhood.

Any woman who is a member of the Women's Building may display her art on the Open Wall Gallery, and the Rental Gallery is rented to women artists for a fee.

The Women's Building is a political place and, as you would expect, most of the exhibitions have a specific point of view, especially in the art/information exhibits. In addition to lectures and studio workshops, video screenings and performances are also offered.

COMMUNITY ART CENTERS

Southern California community art centers offer a combination of visual, performing, and educational art experiences that are directed at local communities but often have a much broader appeal.

Several of these centers have sophisticated gallery spaces featuring art exhibits of interest to general audiences, and just about all of the centers are located near or in historically interesting sites.

The centers, generally operated by a city department, do not charge admission, have free parking, and are accessible to people in wheelchairs. Although all of the centers offer special workshop programs and studio art classes, the following listings focus on art exhibitions.

BRAND LIBRARY AND ART CENTER

1601 West Mountain Street
Glendale, California 91202
(213) 956-2051
HOURS: Tuesday and Thursday, noon to 9 PM; Wednesday, Friday, and Saturday, noon to 6 PM
DIRECTIONS: Take the Golden State Freeway (north) to the Western Avenue exit. Go east on Western to Mountain and up the hill to the center.

Although it looks like a white castle perched high in the foothills overlooking Glendale and the San Fernando Valley, Brand Library is a unique institution that offers a library, exhibition space, and a concert hall.

The library is housed in a remarkable multi-story mansion built by Leslie C. Brand in 1904. The design of the building was inspired by the East Indian Pavillion at the 1836 World Exposition in Chicago. The architecture is primarily Saracenic (from the deserts between Syria and Arabia), with crenellated arches, bulbous domes, and minarets that combine characteristics of Spanish, Moorish, and Indian styles. The interior, in contrast to the cool, elegant exterior, follows Victorian decor and features many fine woods, Tiffany glass, and silk damask. When Mr. Brand died in 1925, he bequeathed "El Miradero," as it was called, to the City of Glendale to be used as a library and park. In 1969, a new wing was added for concerts, lectures, and exhibitions.

LIBRARY. The library collection is devoted to the arts and includes over thirty-two thousand volumes on history, theory, criticism, and techniques. It has an especially large selection of encyclopedias, dictionaries, indexes, and other guides to art, music, and literature. Rare books are not featured, but out-of-print and hard-to-find publications on visual arts and music are available. Although a large portion of the library does not circulate, the library does lend such items as books, cassette tapes, records, librettos, sheet music scores, piano rolls, colored slides, and art prints.

EXHIBITS. The exhibit space includes a large gallery, a glass and concrete sculpture court, and a foyer gallery. Monthly art exhibits featured in the main gallery focus on contemporary traditional art, including National Watercolor Society juried shows and presentations from the Society of Calligraphy. Books, ceramics, and jewelry are featured in the library display cases.

JAPANESE-AMERICAN CULTURAL AND COMMUNITY CENTER

244 South San Pedro
Los Angeles, California 90013
(213) 628-2725
GALLERY HOURS: Hours depend on exhibition; call for specific information.
DIRECTIONS: In downtown Los Angeles, on San Pedro, between Second and Third Streets. From the Harbor Freeway exit at Fourth Street, continue past Broadway to San Pedro and turn left.
PARKING: Street parking.

Located in the heart of Little Tokyo, this center is concerned with serving the Japanese community in Los Angeles and encouraging an understanding of Japan's rich cultural heritage. A large gallery on the first floor of the five-story center, operated by the Japan American Society, presents small exhibits that focus on Japanese art and culture. Recent exhibits include "Image and Life: 50,000 Years of Japanese Prehistory" (an extensive show organized by the Museum of Anthropology at the University of British Columbia), "Three Japanese American Artists," and small sculpture by Isamu Noguchi, who will be designing an elaborate plaza adjacent to the center. The center is also developing an extensive library on Japanese culture.

If possible, ask someone to show you the center's exquisite Japanese Garden, which is barely visible from the street.

MILLS HOUSE VISUAL ARTS COMPLEX

The Village Green in Euclid Park
12732 Main Street
Garden Grove, California
(714) 638-6707
GALLERY HOURS: Wednesday through Sunday, noon to 4 PM
DIRECTIONS: At the junction of the Santa Ana and Garden Grove Freeways. Located on Main Street between Garden Grove Boulevard and Lampson Avenue, adjacent to Euclid Street.

Mills House, established as a gallery in 1974, is part of a cultural complex which also includes the Gem Theater and amphitheater. It is divided into two galleries which are separated by a courtyard. Mills House West, which showcases Orange County artists, was a private residence built in 1922 for the Fulsom family. (It is named for Myrtle Fulsom's grandfather, Andrew Mills, an early California pioneer.) A small gallery in the old house presents changing exhibits every six weeks.

Mills House East, which opened in 1979, is a large rectangular concrete-block structure that mounts three or four major shows each year. Recent exhibits include "Artes de Mexico," featuring Mexican folk art, and "Who's Who That's Who," a multi-media exhibit of celebrated professional artists from Orange County. "Without Limitations" presented the work of blind artists; antique wooden animals were the focus of "Carousel Art;" and American Indian art was featured in "Echoes of the Past."

MUCKENTHALER CULTURAL CENTER

1201 West Malvern Avenue
Fullerton, California 92633
(714) 738-6595
GALLERY HOURS: Tuesday through Sunday, noon to 5 PM
DIRECTIONS: On the corner of Euclid and Malvern. Take the 91 freeway to Fullerton and exit at Euclid Avenue (north). Make a left turn on Malvern at the light and then turn right on Buena Vista to park.

The Muckenthaler Center's Mediterranean-style building was designed as a private home in 1923 for the Muckenthalers, a family that once owned most of the farmland around Fullerton. Situated on eight-and-a-half acres of lawn and gardens, the house includes fixtures and architectural details from Italy. In addition to classes, lectures, and performing arts events, the center offers changing exhibitions every month. Recent shows include "Oriental Cloisonné," "Women Artists of the American West," "Patrick Crabb: Aspects of Ancient Art" (contemporary ceramics), and

"Bali: Morning of the World" (Balinese art). In March, children's art is on exhibit.

PALOS VERDES COMMUNITY ARTS ASSOCIATION

5504 West Crestridge Road
Rancho Palos Verdes, California 90274
(213) 541-2479
HOURS: Tuesday through Friday, 9 AM to 4 PM; Saturday, 11 AM to 2 PM; Sunday, 1 to 4 PM
DIRECTIONS: Take the San Diego Freeway to the Crenshaw exit; the center is at Crenshaw and Crestridge

The Palos Verdes Community Arts Association (PVAA) presents ten major exhibitions each year in its elegant new gallery, as well as monthly shows featuring work by local artists.

In addition to an annual juried show of members' art held each June (a different medium is featured each year) and one exhibit of children's art in May, the center has a specific exhibition policy. In February, the "Collector's Show" features objects from private collections and concentrates on a specific area of art, such as African or American Indian. Artists from one area of the Los Angeles community—La Cienega, Venice, downtown—are highlighted in an annual fall show, and another exhibit presents the work of one (usually well known) Los Angeles artist. During the summer, PVAA has an Artist in Residence program, and the exhibits tend to reflect whatever medium that artist works in. Every other year, the center organizes a special exhibit designed for teenagers.

RIVERSIDE ART CENTER AND MUSEUM

3425 Seventh Street
Riverside, California 92501
(714) 684-7111

HOURS: Tuesday through Saturday, 10 AM to 5 PM; closed in August and for two weeks during Christmas and New Year's

DIRECTIONS: At Seventh and Orange in the heart of Riverside. See Riverside Municipal Museum for freeway directions.

The handsome Main Gallery is the former gymnasium, and the Sales Gallery was once the plunge, but you'd never really guess that this art center and museum is the former Riverside YWCA. And not just any YWCA, but one designed in 1929 by Julia Morgan, the chief architect of Hearst Castle in San Simeon. In addition to the Main Gallery, the two-story Mediterranean-style building houses a children's gallery upstairs and several art studios.

The Main Gallery presents changing exhibits of work by Southern California artists, with an emphasis on those from the Inland Empire—an area that includes Riverside, San Bernardino, and other desert communities. Regional artists are presented in group and solo exhibitions, but artists from all over the state have been represented in special invitationals that focus on a specific medium such as fibers or ceramics.

The museum also has four annual exhibits each year: a members' show in December, the "Purchase Prize Competition" in February/March, the "Watercolor West Exhibit" each April, and the "Riverside All High School Art Exhibit" in June. Unlike most centers, Riverside has dining facilities and a shop. The Atrium Restaurant serves lunch from 11 AM to 2 PM Tuesday through Friday. The sales gallery offers a fine selection of high-quality ceramics, weavings, and art objects by artist/members. All of the pieces for sale are judged by a special selection committee.

VETERANS' MEMORIAL COUNTY PARK CULTURAL ARTS CENTER

13000 Sayre Street
Sylmar, California 91432
(213) 367-1957

HOURS: Tuesday through Friday, noon to 4 PM; Saturday and Sunday, 11 AM to 4 PM

DIRECTIONS: Take the Golden State Freeway to 118 Freeway to 210 Freeway (north). Get off at the Hubbard Street exit and go north on Eldridge, then left to Sayre. Thirty minutes from downtown Los Angeles.

This Cultural Arts Center has the unique distinction of being in the former laundry room of Olive View Hospital—the only building at the Sylmar Veterans' Hospital that survived the 1971 earthquake. Situated in a beautiful 96-acre park, the center offers a spectacular view of the entire San Fernando Valley. It has photography, print, art, and ceramic studios and, like all other centers, offers classes. Exhibitions, which change every four to six weeks, include an annual "Heart of the West" exhibit of contemporary western-style paintings and sculpture. Lapidary exhibits are also of particular interest to the local community. This center has a reputation for mounting small but well-conceived exhibits.

WATTS TOWERS ARTS CENTER AND TOWERS OF SIMON RODIA

1727 East 107th Street
Los Angeles, California 90002
(213) 569-8181

GALLERY HOURS: Monday through Thursday, 9 AM to 5 PM

TOWER HOURS: Parts of the towers are being restored and may be closed to the public. If this is so, they are

still easily viewed from outside. Daylight hours are suggested. Normally open from 10 AM to sundown.
DIRECTIONS: Take the Harbor Freeway (south) to the Century Boulevard exit and turn left. Continue west to Central and turn right, then drive two blocks to 103rd Street, cross the railroad tracks to Graham, and turn right. Proceed four blocks to 107th Street and turn left. Park on Graham.

THE CENTER. The Watts Towers Arts Center is literally in the shadow of the famous Watts Towers, and the hundreds of visitors who flock to the towers each year often miss the center because they are looking up. Although the center emphasizes programs and activities for the local community, it also presents changing exhibits of general interest. For instance, in "The Versatile Rectangle," objects from many cultures, including cooking utensils and ritual artifacts, were displayed.

THE TOWERS. Watts Towers—officially the Towers of Simon Rodia—have been called "the greatest structure ever constructed by one man," "a gigantic flower of folk art," and "a monument to human spirit, energy and skill."

The eight towers are the work of Simon Rodia, an Italian immigrant who built them over a period of thirty-three years, working without drawing board, designs, machine equipment, scaffolding, bolts, rivets, or welds. He created a structure literally "built in the air," using only a tile-setter's simple tools and a window-washer's belt and bucket. Rodia collected over seventy thousand seashells, salvaged thousands of tiles and bottles, and dismantled pipe structures and bedframes which he incorporated into the towers.

The towers, two of which soar over ten stories high, fall into no formal art category, yet they are world-famous. In 1959, delegates attending the Eleventh Assembly of the International Association of Art Critics passed a resolution stating: "We hope every measure will be taken for preservation and upkeep of this structure, a unique combination of sculpture and architecture and a paramount achievement of twentieth-century folk art in the United States."

As it turned out, the towers were deteriorating badly, due to corrosion of the iron framework with a little help from air pollution, natural weathering, and minor earthquakes. The towers have been restored, and although portions of the site may not be open to visitors, the towers are visible from a radius of several blocks.

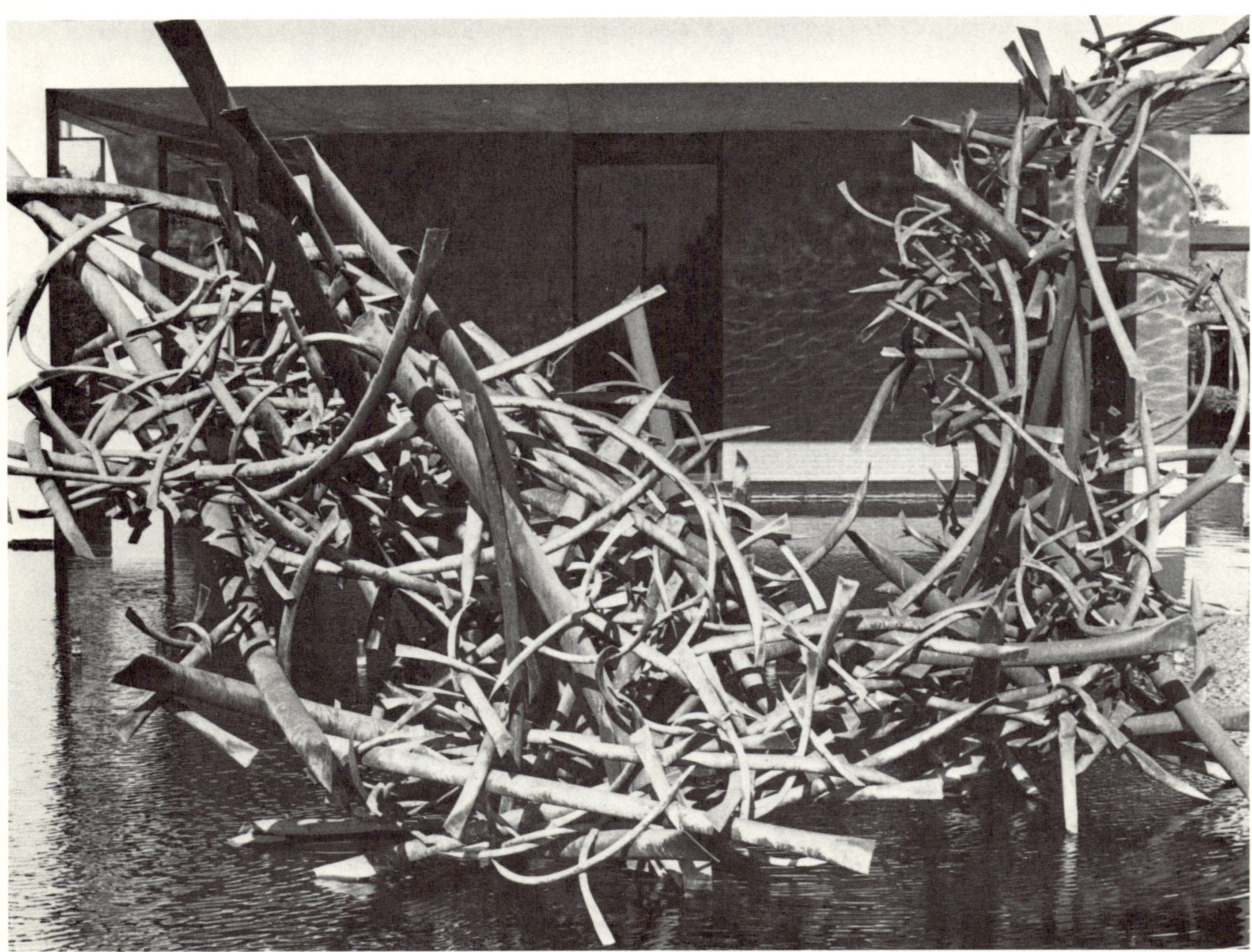

"U" As a Set, Claire Falkenstein
California State University, Long Beach

Whether it be a converted classroom or a sophisticated exhibition hall, just about every college campus has a space designated as an art gallery. University gallery exhibits range from scholarly retrospectives to experimental installation pieces. More than often, these exhibits are innovative, interesting, and important artistic statements.

University galleries do not, as one might imagine, concentrate exclusively on student or faculty art. Most galleries devote very little exhibition space to "in-house" art, and instead present a broad spectrum of ideas and concepts for the benefit of both university and local community.

A majority of these galleries focus on local contemporary art. This is due to the interests of the gallery directors and their desire to complement the art instruction program, as well as to the prohibitive costs of shipping and crating elaborate travelling exhibits.

Geography can play a role in a university gallery's focus. Galleries in remote areas usually assume a more general exhibition policy, while urban galleries often pursue subjects not likely to be presented by other local institutions.

The listings in this section are of institutions which have a reputation for presenting important exhibits, or have unique exhibition policies or specializations. This sampling neglects the numerous fine galleries that concentrate on regional art, since only those institutions with a broader focus were included. Superb regional art is presented at many universities, including Occidental College, the Guggenheim Gallery at Chapman College, the Peppers Gallery at the University of Redlands, Saddleback College (which also has a slide registry of Orange County artists), and the Cypress College Fine Arts Gallery.

College and university galleries are notorious for keeping odd schedules. Most close during quarter or semester breaks, and many shut down for the entire summer. It is advisable to check your local newspaper or call the gallery to confirm hours. A second problem is parking: it is usually difficult to find and is often nowhere near the gallery.

ART CENTER COLLEGE OF DESIGN

1700 Lida Street
Pasadena, California 91103
(213) 577-1700
HOURS: Monday through Thursday, 9 AM to 10 PM; Friday, 9 AM to 5 PM; Saturday, 9 AM to 1 PM; closed when the college is not in session
DIRECTIONS: Located just above the Rose Bowl. From the 210 Freeway, exit at Orange Grove (which turns into Holly), turn right to Linda Vista and then left on Lida Street. From the 134 (which passes through Glendale), take the Linda Vista exit and turn left onto Lida Street.
WHEELCHAIR ACCESS: Yes. Call for specific details.

The Art Center College of Design, housed in a striking bridge-like structure that spans two hills, has two gallery spaces. The Main Gallery features student work, which usually reflects the very high standards required of Art Center students. Exhibits, which change three times each year, feature photography, illustration, fine art, and product design.

The South Gallery presents a number of temporary exhibits designed to complement the programs of the various departments which comprise the college. Exhibits, which feature "names" in each discipline, have included Irving Penn photographs, posters by top Japanese artists, Syd Mead industrial design, illustrations and graphics by Milton Glaser, Paul Davis illustrations, selections from the Robert Rowan Collection of fine arts, and graphic and fine arts by John Massey. One exhibit, organized in Paris, featured the work of top French fashion designers.

Special exhibits are only scheduled during the first half of each trimester because during the second half, the South Gallery is used for large-scale student industrial design projects.

The college also offers free tours of the studios, laboratories, and workshops on Monday and Wednesday at 2 PM throughout the year, and on Friday at 10:30 AM except in August and September.

BROOKS INSTITUTE PHOTOGRAPHIC GALLERY

2020 Alameda Padre Sierra
Santa Barbara, California 93101
(805) 969-2291
HOURS: Monday through Friday, 9 AM to 4 PM
DIRECTIONS: From Highway 101, exit at Mission Street. Drive east until the street dead-ends, turn left, continue for two blocks, and turn right.
WHEELCHAIR ACCESS: No

The Brooks Institute, a school of photographic art and science, has a small gallery devoted to photography. Exhibits have included work by Philippe Halsman, three generations of Weston, and Robert Sission (*National Geographic* staff photographer). A major student show is presented each year.

CALIFORNIA STATE UNIVERSITY, DOMINGUEZ HILLS

University Art Gallery

1000 East Victoria Street
Carson, California 90747
(213) 516-3310
HOURS: Monday through Friday, 11 AM to 5 PM; closed in the summer
DIRECTIONS: From the San Diego Freeway (north), exit at Avalon; going south, exit at Vermont. From the Harbor Freeway (north), exit at Torrance; going south, take the 190th Street off-ramp (190th Street turns into Victoria).
WHEELCHAIR ACCESS: Yes

Although this gallery was only established in 1978, it already has demonstrated a strong commitment to presenting the work of talented West Coast artists. Recent shows have featured Laddie John Dill, John Battenberg, and architectural drawings by A. Quincy Jones. Since there are no other places in the immediate area presenting contemporary art, the gallery is concerned with bringing a variety of contemporary visual art experiences to the community. Exhibits also focus on studio arts offered at the university, including design, ceramics, drawing, and painting.

CALIFORNIA STATE UNIVERSITY, FULLERTON

University Center Gallery

800 North State College Boulevard
Fullerton, California 92634

(714) 733-3262
HOURS: Monday through Friday, noon to 4 PM; Sunday 1
    to 4 PM
DIRECTIONS: From the Orange Freeway (57), exit at Nut-
    wood and drive west to State College Boulevard; turn
    right onto Dorothy Lane and then left into a coin-
    operated parking lot.
WHEELCHAIR ACCESS: Yes

Considered one of the finest university galleries, Cal State
Fullerton's University Center Gallery presents four major
contemporary exhibits each year. Exhibits, organized and
installed as part of the university's museum studies program, are recognized for their outstanding installation design as well as for their content.

The gallery tries to attract different audiences by pre-
senting a combination of general and esoteric shows. Recent exhibits have included "Neon Signs and Symbols;" two
large-scale sculpture installations created by Guy Dill and
Laddie Dill; a twenty-five-square-foot sculpture by Sam
Richardson; "Jewelers U.S.A.," which featured the work of
thirty-five jewelers; ceramics by Mexican artist Juan
Quezada; three-dimensional weavings by New York artist
Claire Zeisler; and kimonos and obi by Itchiku Kubota, a
Japanese artist who revived a special sixteenth-century dye-
ing process.

CALIFORNIA INSTITUTE OF TECHNOLOGY

Baxter Gallery
1201 East California Boulevard
Pasadena, California 91125
(213) 795-6811
HOURS: Daily, noon to 5 PM; closed in the summer.
DIRECTIONS: From Highway 210, exit at Hill Avenue,
    drive south to Del Mar Boulevard, and turn right on
Chester Street. Chester dead-ends into a parking lot
and the gallery is at the southwest corner.
WHEELCHAIR ACCESS: Yes

Despite its somewhat incongruous association with a sci-
ence-oriented institution, the Baxter Gallery is a top-notch
contemporary gallery focusing on American artists. The gallery mounts six major exhibits each year which are well
documented in special catalogues.

Recent exhibits include "Nathan Oliveira: A Survey of
Monotypes, 1973–1978," which traveled to other institutions across the country; "Richard Tuttle;" "Bryan Rogers'
Timepieces;" "Bruce Richards;" "Laddie John Dill
(1971–1976);" and "Trains and Boats and Planes," a mixed-
media exhibit that explored real and fantasy aspects of
travel.

CALIFORNIA STATE UNIVERSITY, LOS ANGELES

Fine Arts Gallery
Fine Arts Building
5154 State University Drive
Los Angeles, California
(213) 224-3521
HOURS: Monday through Thursday, and Sunday, noon to 5
    PM; closed during the summer and on Fridays and Sat-
    urdays
DIRECTIONS: San Bernardino Freeway to the Eastern Av-
    enue exit; turn left directly into the campus.
WHEELCHAIR ACCESS: Yes

This gallery offers a balance of historic and contemporary
exhibitions that are designed to serve the university and the
community. Historic exhibits have included Early American
coverlets and Chinese artifacts. Contemporary exhibits are
not restricted to local artists, and range from photo-realism

to on-site installations and architectural drawings. The gallery organizes eight of the fifteen exhibits it presents each year. A graduate show is scheduled in mid-May. Cal State Los Angeles has another space called the Exploratorium, located in the student union.

CALIFORNIA STATE UNIVERSITY, LONG BEACH

The Art Museum and Galleries

1250 Bellflower Boulevard
Long Beach, California 90804
(213) 498-5761
HOURS: Monday through Thursday from noon to 8 PM
(except 4–5 PM when gallery is closed); Friday, 1–4 PM;
Sunday, 1 to 5 PM.
DIRECTIONS: From the San Diego Freeway, take the Bellflower exit and drive south. The gallery is near Seventh
and Bellflower.
WHEELCHAIR ACCESS: Yes

A commitment to Southern California arts and artists is the hallmark of this gallery, which has an excellent reputation for exhibitions that showcase Southern California artists, especially those from Los Angeles. The recent development of the *Center for Southern California Studies in the Visual Arts* has created an important resource for students, artists, historians, and collectors. The center, a division of the museum, is devoted to the identification, study, preservation, publication, and exhibition of art and visual art resources in Southern California. It concerns itself with art made in California, ranging from Indian baskets and historic photographs to current painting and sculpture.

The center has sponsored several important exhibits, including "Frances Benjamin Johnston: Women of Class and Station," which featured turn-of-the-century photographs; "Thirty Years of Clay: 1949–1979," which was devoted to

the artistic production of the university's graduate alumni; "Käthe Kollwitz," which recreated a 1937 Los Angeles exhibit of this German artist's work; and a print retrospective of Nathan Oliveira.

CALIFORNIA STATE UNIVERSITY, NORTHRIDGE

Fine Art Gallery

Fine Arts Building
18111 Nordhoff
Northridge, California 91330
(213) 885-2226
(213) 885-2210
HOURS: Monday, noon to 4 PM; Tuesday through Friday,
10 AM to 4 PM; closed January, June through August,
and between shows
DIRECTIONS: From the San Diego Freeway (north), exit at
Nordhoff; drive west on Nordhoff for about three
miles. The campus is just east of Reseda Boulevard.
WHEELCHAIR ACCESS: Yes

Exhibits here offer a broad spectrum of visual experiences. The gallery, which features local and international artists in its contemporary shows, also presents non-western art. Recent exhibits have included "Ukiyo-e and the Feminine Mystique," "Americans in Paris: The 50s," and theatre design by Simon Lissim. A faculty show is usually presented in February, while student exhibitions are scheduled for April/May and December.

GALLERIES OF THE CLAREMONT COLLEGES

This complex of several separate colleges has two major galleries: *Montgomery Art Gallery* on the campus of Pomona College, and *Lang Art Gallery* at Scripps College. The two galleries share the same staff, which is responsible for exhibition programs at both spaces, and both galleries have wheelchair access. (714) 621-8000

LANG ART GALLERY
Scripps College
Ninth and Columbus
Claremont, California 91711

MONTGOMERY ART GALLERY
Pomona College
College at Bonita
Claremont, California 91711

HOURS: Daily, 1 to 5 PM; closed during the winter break in January, spring break in mid-March, and during the summer (mid-May to early September)
DIRECTIONS: To reach the Claremont Colleges, take the Indian Hill-Claremont exit of the San Bernardino Freeway and continue north on Indian Hill. For MONTGOMERY ART GALLERY, turn right on Bonita Avenue; for LANG ART GALLERY, take Indian Hill to Tenth Street and then turn right on Columbia Avenue.

The Galleries of the Claremont Colleges present high-quality group exhibits that feature a variety of viewpoints and styles. Recent exhibits have included "Works on Paper 1900–1960 from Southern California Collections," "Paper Art," "Sixteenth-Century Italian Prints," "Black and White are Colors: Paintings of the 1950s–1970s," "Recent Los Angeles Painting," and "Photographs from Life Magazine: The First Decade." About half the exhibits are coordinated in-house, with the balance featuring traveling shows organized by other institutions. The caliber of the exhibitions is high, and they often circulate to other museums. Selections from the galleries' permanent collection—which is especially strong in American Impressionist painting, Native American art (basketry, pottery, and beadwork), and contemporary ceramics—are showcased throughout the year in changing exhibitions.

LOYOLA MARYMOUNT UNIVERSITY

Malone Art Gallery
Loyola Boulevard at West 80th Street
Los Angeles, California 90045
(213) 642-2880
HOURS: Monday through Saturday, 11 AM to 4 PM
DIRECTIONS: From the San Diego Freeway (south), take the La Tijera exit and turn right. Make a right turn on Manchester Boulevard and then another right at Loyola Boulevard, which leads directly into the campus. From the San Diego Freeway (north), exit at La Tijera and turn left; follow the above directions.
WHEELCHAIR ACCESS: Yes

The six or seven exhibits presented in this gallery range from traditional retrospectives to contemporary art. Each academic year, there are several historic exhibits, one or two shows that present unestablished West Coast artists, and, in May, a student exhibit. Recent exhibits have included "Islamic Art," "The Faces of Jesus: Images from the Fifteenth Century to the Present," "Ancient Vase Paintings," and "Picasso Ceramics."

MOUNT ST. MARY'S COLLEGE

Fine Art Gallery
Jose Druos Bieda Art Building
12001 Chalon Road
Los Angeles, California 90049
(213) 476-2237

HOURS: Wednesday through Sunday, noon to 4 PM; closed
in the summer
DIRECTIONS: From the San Diego Freeway, exit at Sunset
Boulevard, drive one mile and turn right on Bundy
Drive. The college is at the top of the hill.
WHEELCHAIR ACCESS: Yes

There is a reason why eighty percent of the people who visit
this gallery, high on a hilltop overlooking West Los Angeles,
are from the community—the exhibits are good. The gallery, which organizes four to five major shows each year, is
especially recognized for its commitment to contemporary
photography. Exhibits have included the first West Coast
show of works by major contemporary European photographers; a show under the curatorship of artist Leland Rice
which featured images of Los Angeles; and "Interchange,"
which explored concerns shared by painters and photographers. The gallery also presents painting exhibits and other
work by West Coast artists.

ORANGE COAST COLLEGE PHOTOGRAPHY GALLERY

Fine Arts Building
2701 Fairview Road
Costa Mesa, California 92626
(714) 556-5629
HOURS: Monday through Friday, 8 AM to 5 PM and 6 to 9
PM.
DIRECTIONS: From the San Diego Freeway, exit at Fair-
view Road and drive south for approximately one
mile.
WHEELCHAIR ACCESS: Yes

Orange Coast College has the largest photography department of any community college in the United States, and

has also developed a reputation for presenting interesting
and innovative exhibits. The nine one-artist shows each
year, organized and installed by students as part of their
academic training, present a balance of local and established
photographs. The exhibits cover all facets of photography
and present documentary photographs as well as experimental photographic processes. A gallery devoted to student work is next to the main exhibition area.

OTIS ART INSTITUTE OF PARSONS SCHOOL OF DESIGN

Art Gallery
2401 Wilshire Boulevard
Los Angeles, California 90057
(213) 387-5288
HOURS: Tuesday through Saturday, 10:30 AM to 5 PM;
Sunday, 1 to 5 PM
DIRECTIONS: From the Santa Monica Freeway, take the
Hoover exit, drive north to Wilshire Boulevard, and
turn right. The institute is at Wilshire and Parkview
Avenue.
WHEELCHAIR ACCESS: Yes

Otis, which recently merged with Parsons School of Design
in New York, is an educational institution for fine art. Exhibits focus on contemporary art by local, national, and
international artists, and have featured the work of Bill
Lundberg and William Wegman, Barry Leva and Bob Ther-
ian, Tom Holste, Guy de Cointet, Steve Lahn, and Anthony
Hernandez. MFA shows are held during December and
April/May; there are juried student sales in December and
April.

SAN DIEGO STATE UNIVERSITY

University Gallery
San Diego, California 92182
(714) 265-6511
HOURS: Tuesday through Saturday, noon to 4 PM; closed in
  the summer
DIRECTIONS: From the San Diego Freeway, exit at College Avenue and follow signs to the gallery. Parking is
  available adjacent to the gallery.
WHEELCHAIR ACCESS: Yes

This gallery tends to emphasize the work of contemporary
California artists. The six exhibits each year, which include
one sponsored by the Art Council, have in the past showcased work by Billy Al Bengston, Ron Davis and the artists
represented by a particular commercial gallery (Janus and
Newspace have been among those featured). A Masters
Gallery in the same art complex presents student shows
and, on occasion, work by faculty members.

UNIVERSITY OF CALIFORNIA, IRVINE

Fine Arts Village
Irvine, California 92717
(714) 833-6610
HOURS: Tuesday through Saturday, noon to 5 PM; closed
  during the summer and between installations
DIRECTIONS: From the San Diego Freeway, take the
  Culver Drive exit (west) to Campus Drive and turn
  right; continue to Bridge Road and turn left to the Fine
  Arts Village.
WHEELCHAIR ACCESS: Yes

This gallery presents high-caliber contemporary art exhibitions which feature local and international artists working in
a variety of media. Ranging from photography to performance, monthly exhibits have featured the work of Craig
Kauffman, John Paul Jones, Max Ernst (tapestries), DeWain
Valentine, and John Cage (an exhibit of mathematics and
sound), and etchings from Crown Point Press. Exhibits often
integrate the work of major artists with that of less established artists, sometimes students, to present a range of
ideas and approaches. UCI, which has an excellent reputation for its studio arts program and attracts well-known
artists to its faculty, also has a space in the back of the gallery
where work by graduate students is exhibited.

UNIVERSITY OF CALIFORNIA, LOS ANGELES

UCLA has four major art spaces: the Frederick S. Wight
Gallery, the Franklin D. Murphy Sculpture Garden, the
Grunwald Graphic Arts Center and the Museum of Cultural
History. All are accessible to wheelchairs.

FREDERICK S. WIGHT ART GALLERY

Dickson Art Center
UCLA
Los Angeles, California 90024
(213) 825-9345; 825-1461
HOURS: Tuesday through Friday, 11 AM to 5 PM; Saturday
  and Sunday, 1 to 5 PM
LOCATION: North end of campus, near Hilgard and
  Sunset.

UCLA is like a small city, so it is not surprising that its gallery
operates more as a museum than as a traditional university
gallery. Founded in 1953, the gallery has been in its present
fourteen-thousand-square-foot exhibition space since 1973.
In addition to four student exhibits each year, the gallery
schedules one major exhibit in cooperation with the UCLA

Museum of Cultural History and another that is sponsored by the UCLA Art Council. This, unfortunately, means that there is little time left on the calendar for other exhibitions, and so the gallery does not organize many shows.

Recent exhibits, excluding those organized by the UCLA Museum of Cultural History, include the work of sculptor Gaston Lachaise; "Medieval Ceramics from the Fourth Through the Eighth Centuries;" monotypes and impressions by Richard Diebenkorn; "Birds, Beasts, Blossoms and Bugs: The Nature of Japan;" "Art about Art," an exhibit organized by the Whitney Museum in New York; "Connections: The Work of Charles and Ray Eames;" and "American Impressionists."

Collections maintained by the gallery, but not on permanent display, include twentieth-century painting and photography and a collection of European paintings from the fifteenth through the nineteenth centuries.

The UCLA Art Council guides conduct free tours of exhibits Tuesday through Saturday at 1:00 PM. The Council also operates a gallery shop which offers a good selection of posters, gift items, and books.

FRANKLIN D. MURPHY SCULPTURE GARDEN

UCLA
At the north end of the campus, near Sunset Boulevard and
    Hilgard Avenue
HOURS: Open at all times

This splendid sculpture garden, beautifully displayed on more than five acres of lawn, features American and European sculpture from the late nineteenth century to the present. It includes major works by Alexander Archipenko, Jean Arp, Emile Antoine Bourdelle, Alexander Calder, Claire Falkenstein, Barbara Hepworth, Jacques Lipchitz, Aristide Maillol, Anna Mahler, Henri Matisse, Joan Miró, Henry Moore, Isamu Noguchi, Auguste Rodin, David Smith, and Francisco Zuñiga.

GRUNWALD CENTER FOR GRAPHIC ARTS AND PRINT GALLERY

Second floor of the Frederick S. Wight Gallery in Dickson
    Art Center
UCLA
Los Angeles, California 90024
(213) 825-3783
HOURS: Tuesday through Friday, 11 AM to 1 PM; Saturday
    and Sunday, 1 to 5 PM—call for an appointment to visit
    the Print Study Room
LOCATION: North end of campus, near Hilgard and
    Sunset

The Grunwald Center for Graphic Arts, established in 1957, has an extremely fine collection of over thirty thousand prints and drawings from the fifteenth century to the present. The collection emphasizes nineteenth- and twentieth-century graphic arts, and is especially strong in the areas of German Expressionism and French Impressionism and in work by major contemporary European and American artists. It also includes an important study archive of extremely fine Japanese woodblock prints that originally belonged to architect Frank Lloyd Wright.

The Grunwald Print Gallery, adjacent to the study room, features changing exhibits that highlight specific areas of the permanent collection. The Center also organizes major exhibits for the Wight Gallery. A recent show was "The Image and the Means," an overview of graphic arts.

MUSEUM OF CULTURAL HISTORY

Haines Hall, Room 2
UCLA (Central quad, near Royce Hall)
Los Angeles, California 90024
(213) 825-4659; 825-4361
HOURS: Wednesday through Sunday, noon to 5 PM

The Museum of Cultural History has a permanent collection of over 120,000 objects of ethnic and folk art representing contemporary, historic, and prehistoric cultures of Africa, Oceania, the Americas, Asia, the Near East, and Europe. Unfortunately, it has only one gallery—albeit a very nice one—which cannot possibly do justice to this fine collection. Exhibits, often organized by graduate students in conjunction with the museum staff, have featured batik of North Java, Zulu beadwork, Santos figures from Guatemala, Yoruba art, and an exhibit about cross-cultural images of women, "Mother, Worker, Ruler, Witch," that featured objects from prehistoric to contemporary times.

Each year, the museum organizes one exhibit for the Wight Gallery, allowing for a larger and more sophisticated exhibition opportunity. These exhibits have featured "Moche Art of Peru," "Dowries of Kutch," "Arts of Ghana," and "Asian Puppets: Wall of the World."

UNIVERSITY OF CALIFORNIA, RIVERSIDE

U.C.R. has three independently operated art spaces: the California Museum of Photography, the Inland Empire Gallery, and the University Art Galleries.
DIRECTIONS: U.C.R. is at the junction of the Pomona
    Freeway (60) and the 91 Freeway

CALIFORNIA MUSEUM OF PHOTOGRAPHY

Watkins House
3701 Canyon Crest Drive
Riverside, California 92521
(714) 787-5924
HOURS: Monday through Saturday, 10 AM to 3 PM
LOCATION: The museum is located at University Avenue
    and Canyon Crest Drive.

This museum, established in 1978, is the largest photographic archive west of the Mississippi and provides a remarkable overview of the history of photography. Used as a major resource for photographic research, teaching, and preservation, it features permanent displays and changing exhibitions.

The Bingham Camera Collection, on permanent display, is one of the most complete collections of cameras and related photographic accessories in the United States. Ranging from *camera obscuras* to sophisticated miniature cameras, the collection includes an 1853 daguerreotype camera; an original 1888 Kodak; Kodaks owned by the Wright brothers; stero, tintype, and folding cameras; early Exactas; and a 1930 Leica.

Changing exhibits generally feature photographs from the permanent collection, which includes works ranging from the pioneering days of photographic history to examples of recent dye-transfer work.

The collection contains images made in the Near East and Far East during the mid-nineteenth century, photographs that recorded the western expansion of the United States, and the works of major twentieth-century photographers. The Setzer–Alexander Friends of Photography Collection includes six hundred prints by such masters as Ansel Adams, Wynn Bullock, Edward and Brett Weston, Albert Renger-Patzsch, and Adam Clark Vroman.

The Walker Evans Print Study Collection includes sixty prints by this master photographer who is best known for his photo-documentation of the South and his works for *Fortune Magazine*.

The Keystone–Mast Stereographic Collection presents an incredible overview of the stereoscope, with over 350,000 negatives and cards that create a three-dimensional illusion.

INLAND EMPIRE GALLERY

Bannock Burn Complex
3663 A Canyon Crest Drive
Riverside, California 92507
(714) 787-4636
HOURS: Tuesday through Saturday, 11 AM to 3 PM
LOCATION: Bannock Burn Complex is an apartment and shopping complex at Canyon Crest, across from the University.

This small gallery, partially sponsored by UC Riverside student fees, is a cooperative of students, alumni, faculty, and local artists. Established in 1973, the Inland Empire Gallery is member-supported and features work by member-artists in biweekly exhibits. Selected by a special committee, exhibits display the work of one artist, except in December, when there is a group show. Objects on display are for sale.

FINE ART GALLERY

Humanities–Art Building
Riverside, California 92521
(714) 787-4636
HOURS: Monday through Friday, 10 AM to 3 PM; closed in the summer

The Fine Art Gallery presents a wide range of visual art experiences that enrich both the university and the general community. Each year, the gallery presents one historic exhibit (such as etchings by Canaletto), one photography show, and one exhibit of the work of a major contemporary artist. Exhibits also feature paintings and graphics. There is a general student show at the end of the spring quarter.

UNIVERSITY OF CALIFORNIA, SAN DIEGO

Mandeville Art Gallery
Mandeville Center (Room 101)
Muir College
La Jolla, California 92093
(714) 452-2864
HOURS: Sunday through Friday, noon to 5 PM; Wednesday, 7 to 9 PM
DIRECTIONS: Take the Gennesee Avenue exit or the La Jolla Village Drive exit off Highway 5. The gallery is located in the center of the UC San Diego Campus.
WHEELCHAIR ACCESS: Yes

This gallery, located in the center of the UCSD campus, presents changing exhibits that emphasize contemporary art by established artists. The gallery does not present local artists except by invitation in a special group exhibit.

Recent exhibits include Tom Wudl; Frida Kahlo; "L.A. Women/Narrations;" "Micro-Sculpture" (nine artists from the east and west coasts); "Douglas Heubler/Recent Works" (conceptual art); "Betye Saar: Assemblages and Collages;" "Autochromes from the Albert Kahn Collection/Tonkin 1915–1916;" "The Decorative Impulse;" "Miriam Shapiro/The Computer;" "The Shrine and the Doll House;" and "Artists Books Show."

An annual MFA show is scheduled during the spring in the Mandeville Annex Gallery.

UNIVERSITY OF CALIFORNIA, SANTA BARBARA

Art Museum
Arts Complex
Santa Barbara, California 93106
(805) 961-2951
HOURS: Tuesday through Saturday, 10 AM to 4 PM; Sunday, 1 to 5 PM
DIRECTIONS: UCSB is in Goleta, several miles north of downtown Santa Barbara. From Highway 101, take the UC Santa Barbara off-ramp directly to the campus.
WHEELCHAIR ACCESS: Yes

The UCSB Art Museum presents changing exhibits and also features several permanent collections.

Each year, the museum organizes seven or eight major exhibits, including one on architecture and one concerned with a non-western tradition. Recent shows have included "Richard Diebenkorn Intaglio Prints 1961–1968;" "Arp on Paper;" painting and sculpture by Bay Area artists; "In her Image," a cross-cultural show focusing on motherhood of the gods; "The Play Between Rational and High Art," which featured the work of California architect Gregory Ain; and "The Great Goddess in Indian Asia and the Madonna in Christian Culture."

The museum's permanent collection includes an extremely fine selection of architectural drawings that emphasize the work of Southern California architects. The collection, often featured in changing exhibits, may be seen, by appointment, in the study room. The museum also has a large collection of European and American graphics from the seventeenth through the nineteenth centuries which may be seen in the study room. The Morgen Roth Medal Collection, on permanent display, features Baroque and Renaissance bronze medals and plaquettes. Selections from the Sedgwick Collection of fifteenth- and sixteenth-century Dutch and Flemish paintings are rotated throughout the year in one gallery.

UNIVERSITY OF SOUTHERN CALIFORNIA

The Fisher Gallery
Harris Hall
823 Exposition Boulevard
Los Angeles, California
(213) 743-2799
HOURS: Monday through Friday, noon to 5 PM
DIRECTIONS: From the Santa Monica Freeway, take the Vermont exit south to Exposition Boulevard and turn left. The gallery is one-and-one-half blocks east of Vermont on the north side of Exposition.
WHEELCHAIR ACCESS: Yes

The Fisher Gallery presents exhibitions which tend to emphasize contemporary art and architecture. Recent shows include "Reality of Illusion: National Survey of Recent Illusionistic Paintings, Sculpture and Objects;" an in-depth survey of the work of Los Angeles artist Walter Askin; and the "Southern California Photographic Invitational," which presented work by contemporary photographers. Undergraduate art and architecture students exhibit their work each May.

In addition to changing exhibitions, this gallery has several permanent collections. The Elizabeth Holes Fisher Collection, exhibited two times each year, features seventeenth- through nineteenth-century European, British, and American paintings; the Armand Hammer Collection of sixteenth- through nineteenth-century European paintings is on permanent display.

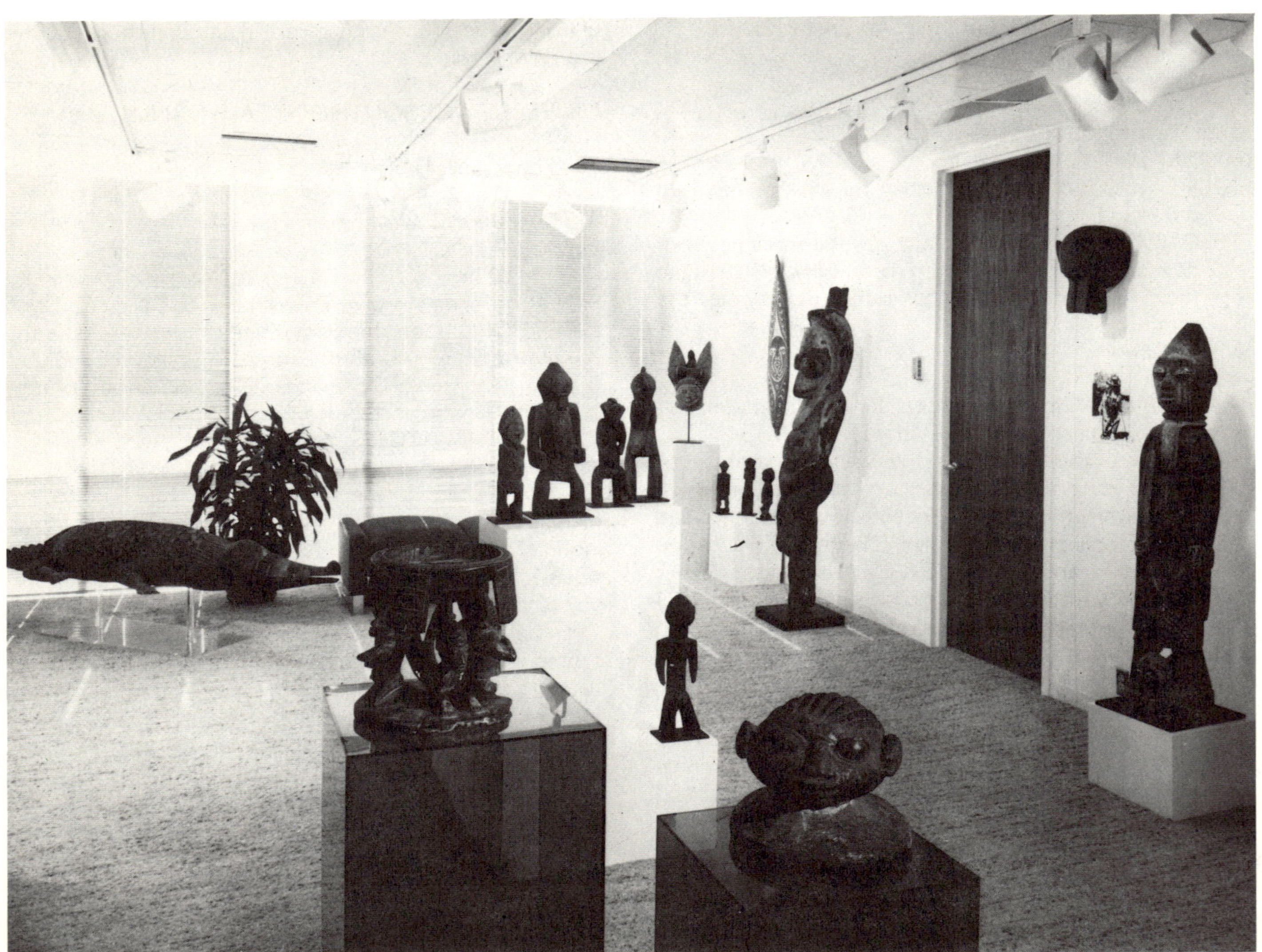

Harry A. Franklin Gallery, Beverly Hills

A commercial gallery, by definition, buys and sells art for profit. Some commerical galleries are nonprofit enterprises, but this is usually unintentional. And while sound financial practice is critical to their success, the similarity of commercial galleries to any other profit-oriented enterprise ends there.

Serious art is not a commodity like shoes or refrigerators. Serious collectors do not buy art to match the living room decor—they buy a visual and emotional experience, a new idea, a piece of history, a mirror of culture. Commercial galleries specialize in collections that run the gamut from ancient artifacts to avant-garde art.

Galleries can be owned and directed by one or several people; sometimes a gallery has a silent financial partner and is directed by someone else. Galleries that survive—and the mortality rate, especially in Los Angeles, is high—are directed and/or owned by people who have good eyes, good instincts, and good business acumen.

People who buy and sell are known as dealers. Many dealers do not have public spaces or galleries, and these "private" dealers have not been included in this publication, since they inhabit another realm of the art world, primarily serving wealthy collectors and museums.

EXHIBITIONS

Exhibits are a small facet of any gallery operation; they are the public face of a gallery's private dealings. Major sales frequently occur before an exhibit formally opens, after it closes, or without any exhibition at all. Exhibits are a ritual—a public service which, while not required, is expected. An exhibition gives the public an opportunity to see the art, and provides the artist with visibility and the gallery with publicity.

One should not automatically assume that an art object is no longer available because an exhibit has closed. If the painting or sculpture has not been sold, the dealer very likely will still have it—or if not, and if the work is by a contemporary artist, the dealer can get in touch with the artist. Of course, the possibility always exists that something will be sold before you make up your mind. Photographs and fine prints, however, are usually available, since more than one copy of the image is created. If something you desire is no longer available, talk with the gallery director; he or she may have other pieces by the same artist from the same period that might interest you.

TO BUY OR NOT TO BUY. When visiting any commercial gallery, you need not feel obliged to create the impression that you are in the market to buy. Since most people do not walk into a gallery, see something they like, and plunk down several hundred or several thousand dollars, galleries do not expect to sell to casual visitors. In fact, regular clients will make an appointment to view an exhibit during non-public hours, to be assured of the dealer's undivided attention. Most galleries are open by special appointment in addition to their regular business hours.

Therefore, gallery browsing not only is acceptable, but is generally encouraged. Galleries that do not want casual visitors will be open by appointment only or will be located in out-of-the-way places like high-rise office buildings. (Even these galleries are pleased to admit non-buyers who appreciate art; they just want to avoid street traffic.)

Most gallery people are pleased to see other people come into their spaces. The chilly, foreboding quality of many galleries is often an unintentional extension of the stark white walls. This unwelcoming atmosphere can be compounded by the absence of other visitors. Some galleries, however, go to great lengths to maintain a distance with anyone they do not know. Once you overcome the somewhat disquieting feeling that you are being ignored, you will enjoy the peaceful experience of viewing the art without being pestered by overly eager sales people.

You will discover that most gallery directors and their staffs are more than happy to answer questions about what is on display. If you don't quite know what to ask, start by inquiring about the artist or the period of art on display.

Reputable galleries will not, under any circumstances, use hard-sell tactics, pressure you to buy, or make crass ''deals'' on the spot. Though it is beyond the scope of this book to discuss the practices of buying art, it is worth noting that many galleries will sell an object on time, often with no interest.

For the purposes of this book, galleries are divided into the following categories: contemporary, traditional, photographic, special focus, and art-related enterprises. The index at the back of the book lists each gallery according to its geographic location.

CONTEMPORARY GALLERIES

Contemporary galleries, perhaps more than any other type of gallery, have a purpose beyond buying and selling of art. They play an important role in presenting and defining current art trends, and, in many ways, are the pulse of the art community.

A contemporary gallery is a complex endeavor that hinges on a delicate, symbiotic relationship between the artist and the gallery owner. The gallery supports and nurtures an artist, both financially and emotionally; but dealers have also been known to take advantage of artists.

Operating a contemporary gallery can be a lucrative but time-consuming and uncertain business. It involves being part of the art community—recognizing artistic potential, taking a risk, ''making'' an artist, being a force behind the creative force.

In order to combine artistic interest with financial security, most galleries will balance shows that feature established artists, whose works are sure to sell, with shows that present new artists or experimental ideas. In presenting new artistic concepts, the ideal is to take a risk that leads to commercial success. A few galleries, however, sometimes present installation pieces or performance events that will not generate any money.

Ask a contemporary gallery director to describe the characteristics of the art he or she represents, and invariably the answer will be ''excellent quality,'' ''new ideas,'' ''challenging concepts.'' Since these galleries are dealing with a number of artists whose ideas are changing and evolving, it is difficult to describe a gallery accurately aside from the personality of the director or the physical characteristics of the space. Gallery spaces tend to be variations of white walls—some spectacular, others merely adequate. The best way to judge a contemporary gallery is by (1) the artists it represents (referred to as a ''stable''), (2) the quality of the work it displays (you can, for example, find galleries that show poor works by great artists), and (3) the risks a gallery is willing to take in terms of presenting new ideas. A "big name" gallery that shows only major established artists serves quite a different function than a small but reputable gallery that concentrates on unknown or emerging artists.

On the surface, Los Angeles may appear to have a plethora of contemporary galleries. Unfortunately, it can boast of only a few important ones. This guidebook presents a list of Los Angeles galleries which have established reputations for showing high-quality, interesting, and exciting contemporary art. The selection is based on an informal survey of people within the art community—gallery owners, art critics, artists, and museum professionals—who were asked, "Which contemporary galleries in the Los Angeles area do you consider to be the most significant?" This listing is the concensus of their answers. It is not an endorsement of the galleries listed, nor should it be considered exhaustive. Use the list as a guide to exploring and let your own experience inform you.

To understand and appreciate the development of contemporary art in Southern California, suggested readings include *Sunshine Muse* by Peter Plagens (published by Praeger in 1974), and museum and gallery catalogues, beginning in the late 1950s.

ACE GALLERY

185 Windward Avenue
Venice, California 90291
(213) 392-4931
HOURS: Tuesday through Saturday, 10 AM to 5 PM
LOCATION: In a former bank building at the corner of
    Windward and Main

Ace, one of the few internationally recognized galleries in Los Angeles, represents major contemporary American artists. It was established in 1961 by Doug Christmas and presents exhibitions of the following artists: Carl Andre, Anthony Caro, Dan Flavin, Sam Francis, Helen Frankenthaler, Michael Heizer, Jasper Johns, Donald Judd, Ellsworth Kelly, Roy Lichtenstein, Robert Mangold, Robert Motherwell, Bruce Nauman, Kenneth Noland, Claes Oldenburg, Larry Poons, Roland Reiss, Robert Rauschenberg, James Rosenquist, Edward Ruscha, Richard Serra, Tony Smith, Frank Stella, Jim Turrell, Cy Twombly, and Andy Warhol.

A visit to Ace is akin to visiting a museum (and many museums buy from Ace) because (1) the pieces are extremely expensive, and (2) some of the installations are not marketable and are shown as more of a public service.

Ace recently opened a second space at 8373 Melrose Avenue, Los Angeles, California 90069.

ASHER/FAURE GALLERY

8221 Santa Monica Boulevard
Los Angeles, California 90046
(213) 654-6214
HOURS: Tuesday through Saturday, 11 AM to 5 PM
LOCATION: Near Crescent Heights Boulevard, in West
    Hollywood

Betty Asher and Pat Faure generally present exhibits that have been assembled by major New York and European dealers. This creates an unusual opportunity to see artists not shown in Los Angeles. Exhibits include twentieth-century and contemporary masters, established American and European artists, and young American painters and sculptors from the East Coast. The gallery does represent several Southern California artists, and these include Paul Dillon, Kathryn Halbower, Michael McMillen, Natasha

Nicholsen, John Okulick, Gwynn Murrill, Elaine Carhart, Nicholas Africano, and Li-Lan.

JAN BAUM–IRIS SILVERMAN GALLERY

8225 Santa Monica Boulevard
Los Angeles, California 90046
(213) 656-8225
HOURS: Tuesday through Saturday, 11 AM to 5 PM
LOCATION: Near Crescent Heights

This gallery, established in 1976, has two distinct specializations: primitive art and contemporary art. The contemporary exhibits for which it is recognized feature emerging California artists, including Peter Plagens, Raymond Saunders, Claude Kent, and Bob Nugent. The primitive exhibits run concurrently with the contemporary shows and focus on African, Tibetan, Oceanic, and Nepalese art. Recent primitive exhibits have been organized around themes such as "Doors and Locks of West Africa and Indonesia," "Non-Ritual African Art," and "Mother and Child in African Art."

CIRRUS GALLERY

542 South Alameda
Los Angeles, California 90013
(213) 680-3473
HOURS: Tuesday through Friday, 11 AM to 5 PM; Saturday, noon to 4 PM
LOCATION: In downtown Los Angeles at Second and Alameda Streets, in a converted warehouse. (Enter around the side.)

Cirrus, one of the first galleries to relocate in downtown Los Angeles, is both a print publisher and a gallery. Established in 1970 by Jean Milant, Cirrus publishes prints by such major artists as Ed Ruscha, Bruce Nauman, Joe Goode, Craig Kauffman, Chris Burden, Vega Celmins, Judy Chicago, and John Baldessari. The gallery, in addition to presenting Cirrus Edition artists, exhibits work by Charles Christopher Hill, Jay McCafferty, Jay Willis, Michael Brewster, Terry O'Shea, and Eugene Steurman.

JAMES CORCORAN GALLERY

8223 Santa Monica Boulevard
Los Angeles, California 90046
(213) 656-0662
HOURS: Tuesday through Friday, 11 AM to 5 PM; Saturday, noon to 5 PM
LOCATION: In West Hollywood, near Crescent Heights.

Each of the major New York and California artists represented by the Corcoran Gallery is featured in a solo exhibit approximately once every eighteen months. Artists include Charles Arnoldi, Don Bachardy, Joanna Beall, Billy Al Bengston, John Baldessari, Tony Berlant, Richard Diebenkorn, Laddie John Dill, Sam Francis, Joseph Goldyne, Marvin Hardin, Ed Moses, David Novros, Ken Price, and Paul Wonner. The Corcoran Gallery is highly regarded by the local art community.

KIRK DE GOOYER GALLERY

830 South Central Avenue
Los Angeles, California 90021
(213) 623-8333
HOURS: Tuesday through Sunday, 11 AM to 5 PM
LOCATION: Between Eighth Street and Olympic Boulevard in downtown Los Angeles.

Although this gallery is very new—it opened in May 1980—it

has quickly become part of downtown Los Angele's emerging art scene. Kirk DeGooyer exhibits large-scale paintings and sculpture by contemporary artists from the western United States, as well as some photography.

ROSAMUND FELSEN GALLERY

669 North La Cienega Boulevard
Los Angeles, California 90069
(213) 652-9172
HOURS: Tuesday through Saturday, 11 AM to 5:30 PM
LOCATION: Between Melrose Avenue and Santa Monica
   Boulevard.

This new gallery has a solid reputation for presenting sculpture, painting, and photography by emerging or recently established artists from Southern California, especially Los Angeles. Gallery artists include Chris Burden, Karen Carson, Ron Cooper, Guy de Cointet, Richard Jackson, Steve Kahn, Peter Lodata, Grant Mudford, Maria Mordman, Leland Rice, Allen Ruppersberg, Alexis Smith, Keith Sonnier, and Ann Thornycroft.

GEMINI G.E. L.

8365 Melrose Avenue
Los Angeles, California 90069
(213) 651-0513
HOURS: Monday through Friday, 9:30 AM to 5:30 PM
LOCATION: On Melrose just east of La Cienega, in West
   Hollywood

Gemini G.E.L. (Graphics Editions Limited) publishes fine graphic editions by contemporary superstars such as Robert Rauschenberg, David Hockney, Jasper Johns, Claes Oldenburg, Sam Francis, Ellsworth Kelly, and Roy Lichtenstein. Established in 1966 by Sidney Felsen and Stanley Grinstein,

Gemini in effect gives its space and master printers over to the artists. Gemini supports the operation and markets the prints.

Gemini's public space is limited to one gallery, basically the reception area, which displays the most recent work it has published. An upstairs gallery features an inventory of past editions, but visitors must be accompanied by a Gemini staff member. (It is best to call ahead.)

JANUS GALLERY

8000 Melrose Avenue
Los Angeles, California 90046
(213) 655-2694
HOURS: Tuesday through Saturday, 11 AM to 5:30 PM
LOCATION: Between La Cienega and La Brea.

Janus, which just moved to this new location from Venice, concentrates on major West Coast artists and presents work by Larry Bell, Craig Kauffman, Lita Albuquerque, Joel Bass, Ed Moses, Guy Dill, Margaret Omar, and Gloria Kisch. This gallery, owned by Jan Turner, also exhibits photography.

L.A. LOUVER

55 North Venice Boulevard
Venice, California 90291
(213) 396-6633
HOURS: Tuesday through Saturday, noon to 6 PM
LOCATION: Just west of Pacific Avenue, south of
   Windward.

L.A. Louver concentrates on paintings, sculpture, and drawings by California artists, but also is known for presenting contemporary British painters. Artists include Max

Cole, Charles Garabedian, Frederick Hammersley, Loren Madsen, John Sturgeon, Don Suggs, Paula Sweet, David Trowbridge, William Brice, and Sandra Berman. Works from the Wallace Berman Estate and the work of David Hockney are also available. In addition, this gallery has a large inventory of graphic works from Petersberg Press and the Crown Point Press. Periodically, L.A. Louver presents historical exhibitions such as ''The Great Knot,'' which featured paintings and drawings by British artists and the work of Kate Steinmetz. Directors: Peter Goulds and Fred Hoffman.

MARGO LEAVIN GALLERY

812 North Robertson Boulevard
Los Angeles, California 90069
(213) 273-0604
HOURS: Tuesday through Saturday, 11 AM to 5 PM
LOCATION: One-half block north of Santa Monica Boulevard.

Margo Leavin, one of the most respected galleries in Los Angeles, features contemporary American art, including graphics, drawings, paintings, and sculpture. It exhibits the work of the following artists: Arakawa, Jennifer Bartlett, Lynda Benglis, Jud Fine, Jim Dine, Charles Gaines, Ann McCoy, Robert Moscowitz, Agnes Martin, Louise Nevelson, Bryan Hunt, Claes Oldenburg, Edda Renouf, Gary Stephen, Lucas Samaras, Hap Tivey, Hannah Wilke, and Tom Wudl. Prints and drawings by the above artists are available in addition to works by Marcel Duchamp, Sam Francis, David Hockney, Joe Goode, Jasper Johns, Ellsworth Kelly, Andy Warhol, James Rosenquist, Roy Lichtenstein, Ed Ruscha, Frank Stella, Robert Motherwell, Robert Rauschenberg, George Segal, John Levee, and Gio Pomodoro. The gallery will often search for a major work on request.

MEKLER GALLERY

651 North La Cienega
Los Angeles, California 90069
(213) 659-0583
HOURS: Tuesday through Saturday, 11 AM to 5 PM
LOCATION: Between Melrose and Santa Monica.

This gallery, while not on the cutting edge of the art scene, exhibits contemporary art with an emphasis on sculpture. Artists include Robert Cremean, William Dole, Sorel Etrog, Dimitri Hadzi, Ynez Johnston, Jack Zajac, and the estate of Rico Lebrun. Exhibits of works by Matisse and Giacometti have also been presented here. Adam Mekler is the director.

MIZUNO GALLERY

210 East Second Street
Los Angeles, California 90013
(213) 625-2491
HOURS: Tuesday through Friday, noon to 5 PM; Saturday, noon to 3 PM
LOCATION: In Little Tokyo between Los Angeles and San Pedro Streets, across from the New Otani Hotel.

Riko Mizuno was a major force on the gallery scene in the 1960s and just recently reopened her gallery in downtown Los Angeles. It is a very small gallery that exhibits paintings and sculpture by American artists, including James Hayward, John Miller, Douglas Wheeler, and Sam Francis.

NEWSPACE

5241 Melrose Avenue
Los Angeles, California 90038

(213) 469-9353
HOURS: Tuesday through Saturday, 11 AM to 4 PM; closed
    in August
LOCATION: In Hollywood, at Van Ness and Melrose.

Newspace, established by Joni Gordon in 1975, exhibits paintings and sculpture by emerging Los Angeles artists. Newspace artists include Martha Alf, Bob Bates, Michael Falzone, Christopher Georgesco, Sidney Gordin, Tom Holste, Paul Knotter, Brian Miller, Marjorie Nodelman, Barney O'Brien, Jon Peterson, Jap Phillips, Astrid Preston, Jeff Price, Bruce Richards, Laura Rothstein, and Wafe Saunders.

ORLANDO GALLERY

14553 Ventura Boulevard
Sherman Oaks, California 91403
(213) 789-6012
HOURS: Tuesday through Saturday, 10 AM to 4 PM
LOCATION: Between Vesper Avenue and Van Nuys Boulevard.

Orlando presents works by Southern California artists, with an emphasis on those from Los Angeles. It also has a small selection of African sculptures and Art Deco objects. The gallery, established in 1961, is concerned with introducing new artists. Two one-artist exhibits run concurrently and part of the gallery regularly features gallery artists or the work of new artists.

NEIL G. OVSEY GALLERY

13814 Ventura Boulevard
Second Floor
Sherman Oaks, California 91403

(213) 788-5382
HOURS: Tuesday through Saturday, 11 AM to 5:30 PM
LOCATION: Two blocks west of Woodman Avenue.

This is the only gallery that specializes exclusively in original lithographs, silkscreens, and etchings by major contemporary artists. In addition to changing exhibits which highlight one or two artists, Ovsey's has a large inventory of prints by Ed Ruscha, Jasper Johns, Claes Oldenburg, Robert Rauschenberg, Joe Goode, Sol LeWitt, William Crutchfield, Eric Orr, David Hockney, Andy Warhol, and Roy Lichtenstein.

The Ovsey gallery recently opened a second space at 701 East Third Street in downtown Los Angeles, at the corner of Alameda and Third Street. It will feature sculpture and paintings as well as multiple images.

SPACE

6015 Santa Monica Boulevard
Los Angeles, California 90038
(213) 461-8166
HOURS: Tuesday through Saturday, 11 AM to 5 PM
LOCATION: In West Hollywood, at Santa Monica and
    Beechwood.

Space is concerned with promoting new artists. Established by Ed Lau in 1975, it usually presents work that is simple, subtle, and very often involves social commentary. Artists include Masami Teraoka, Robert Anderson, Phyllis Davidson, Michael Davis, Seiji Kunishima, Ann Page, and Boyd Rushton Wright. The ambience in this gallery is especially nice, and Space has demonstrated a concern for the artistic community by presenting performances, films, and concerts.

TORTUE GALLERY

2917 Santa Monica Boulevard
Santa Monica, California 90404
(213) 828-8878
HOURS: Tuesday through Saturday, 11 AM to 5:30 PM
LOCATION: In Santa Monica, at 29th Street and Santa
Monica Boulevard.

Tortue presents a balance of young California artists and established blue-chip artists, most of whom work in minimal abstraction. There is a sculpture court behind the two-story gallery, and one small gallery on the first floor is devoted to artists' books. Tortue, which was established in 1969, has a large inventory in its upstairs gallery, with works by David Bottini, Sam Francis, Ed Kienholtz, Tom Leeson, Stanton MacDonald-Wright, John McCracken, Allan McCollum, and Mark Tobey. Gallery artists include Karl Benjamin, Jerry Byrd, Edie Ellis Danieli, Willard Dixon, Martin Facey, Claire Falkenstein, S. W. Hayter, Patrick Hogan, Shirley Pettibone, Greg Renfrow, David Schirm, Stephen Seemayer, Michael Todd, and Joyce Treiman. Tortue also represents the estate of John Altoon. The gallery is expanding to include master drawings by European and American painters, including Degas, Matisse, and Picasso. Director: Mallory Freeman.

TRADITIONAL/HISTORICAL GALLERIES

This section presents a selection of galleries that specialize in traditional European and American art from the eighteenth, nineteenth, and early twentieth centuries. It also features galleries that offer master prints and drawings.

These galleries generally do not have an on-going series of changing exhibitions; instead, they display objects from their inventories and rearrange the galleries three or four times a year.

While most of the galleries sell to private collectors and occasionally to museums, do not let their somewhat formal atmosphere and expensive price lists discourage you from browsing. Since most of the galleries specialize in a particular period of art, the dealers and staff are knowledgable and usually more than happy to answer questions. Galleries that specialize in prints and drawings, because they offer works of art less expensive than paintings, are especially willing to help novice collectors.

BILTMORE GALLERY

515 South Olive Street
Los Angeles, California 90013
(213) 624-6963
HOURS: Monday through Friday, 10:30 AM to 6 PM
LOCATION: In the Biltmore Hotel, between Fifth and
Sixth Streets in downtown Los Angeles, just across
from Pershing Square.

The Biltmore Gallery is the oldest gallery in Los Angeles, and was established in 1924 by a group of artists. Today it specializes in western art, with an emphasis on the Hudson River School (landscapes), the Taos School, and American Impressionism. The art ranges in date from 1850 through 1940, and exhibitions change every four months.

BOWATER GALLERY

769 North La Cienega Boulevard
Los Angeles, California 90069
(213) 655-3723
HOURS: Monday through Saturday, 11 AM to 5 PM
LOCATION: Between Melrose and Santa Monica

Marian Bowater, who established this gallery in 1975, offers late nineteenth-century and early twentieth-century American painting and specializes in California artists of this period.

FEINGARTEN GALLERIES

8380 Melrose Avenue
Los Angeles, California 90069
(213) 655-4840
HOURS: Tuesday through Friday, 11 AM to 5 PM
LOCATION: One block east of La Cienega Boulevard on
    Melrose

Charles Feingarten, who has been a dealer for thirty years, specializes in sculpture by major late-nineteenth- and twentieth-century artists, including Arp, Archipenko, Maillot, Moore, Rodin, Picasso, Giacometti, and Renoir. The gallery also represents a few contemporary artists.

WILLIAM AND VICTORIA DAILEY

8216½ Melrose Avenue
Los Angeles, California 90069
(213) 658-8515
HOURS: Tuesday through Friday, 10 AM to 6 PM; Saturday,
    11 AM to 5 PM
LOCATION: Between La Cienega and Crescent Heights.

This gallery specializes in nineteenth-century French prints by artists such as Géricault, Manet, and Lepere. Although the Daileys deal primarily with museums and established collectors, they are interested in helping new collectors. The gallery, established in 1974, is also known for carrying works by Whistler, Japanese prints, and nineteenth-century European prints influenced by Japanese prints. Art reference books pertaining to the artists and period represented are also available. Special exhibits are presented about six times a year, including an annual fall show of Japanese prints. Other exhibits have featured Daumier, Whistler and his contemporaries, and the invention of lithography. Catalogues are sometimes published to accompany exhibits.

GOLDFIELD GALLERY

8400 Melrose Avenue
Los Angeles, California 90069
(213) 651-1122
HOURS: Monday through Friday, 10 AM to 5 PM; Saturday,
    11 AM to 3 PM
LOCATION: Two blocks east of La Cienega Boulevard, at
    Orlando.

This gallery, established in 1964, offers American art from 1880 through the 1930s, with an emphasis on western American Impressionism and the Taos School. The works of major American painters such as Reginald Marsh and Thomas Hart Benton are also available. Theme exhibits have included "American Landscapes (1850-1950)" and "Women as Subject Matter in American Art." An annex two doors away features contemporary artists.

HERBERT B. PALMER AND CO. GALLERY

9570 Wilshire Boulevard
Suite 430
Beverly Hills, California 90212
(213) 550-7225
HOURS: Tuesday through Friday, 10 AM to 6 PM; Saturday,
    11 AM to 4 PM
LOCATION: On Wilshire Boulevard in Beverly Hills, near
    Camden Drive.

This gallery features the work of contemporary European and American masters—including Henry Moore, Archipenko, Calder, Maillot, and Bonnard—as well as vintage photographs. Established in 1965, it also sells works by northwest American painters such as Morris Graves and a few by established California artists such as Billy Al Bengston.

MARILYN PINK MASTER PRINTS AND DRAWINGS

817 North La Cienega Boulevard
Los Angeles, California 90069
(213) 657-5810
HOURS: Tuesday through Friday, noon to 5 PM; Saturday,
    2:30 to 5 PM
LOCATION: Between Melrose Avenue and Santa Monica
    Boulevard.

Sixteenth- through early twentieth-century drawings and old master prints are the focus of the Pink Gallery. Ms. Pink also sells sporting prints and botanical prints and represents the estate of Louis Lozowick. Recent exhibits have featured images of New York, color prints from the eighteenth through twentieth centuries, and Pierre Bonnard drawings.

ZEITLIN AND VER BRUGGE

815 North La Cienega Boulevard
Los Angeles, California 90069
(213) 652-0784 or 655-7581
HOURS: Monday through Friday, 9 AM to 5 PM; ring bell to
    be admitted or call for an appointment.
LOCATION: Between Melrose Avenue and Santa Monica
    Boulevard.

This gallery, located in the loft of the Zeitlin and ver Brugge Bookstore, specializes in nineteenth- and twentieth-century European and American prints and drawings. It has a small selection of western and California paintings and watercolors from this period, botanical and bird prints (including some by Audubon), and a selection of Currier & Ives maps. For information on the bookstore, please see the listing under commercial enterprises.

SPECIAL-FOCUS GALLERIES

A number of galleries specialize in a particular period, culture, or art form. Specialized galleries are less likely than contemporary galleries to present a series of scheduled exhibitions. They also tend to keep a lower profile, and to rely on collectors who have a specific interest in the area represented.

There is, however, a distinction between galleries that operate exhibition spaces and those that function as stores selling merchandise. For instance, Oriental carpet and antique stores are not considered galleries, even if the quality of their merchandise is excellent. This distinction becomes rather fuzzy in the area of fine crafts; in this guidebook, stores that sell ceramics, handmade jewelry, and other craft items have not been included unless they operate as regular galleries.

HARRY A. FRANKLIN GALLERY

9601 Wilshire Boulevard
Suite 728
Beverly Hills, California 90210
(213) 271-9171
HOURS: Tuesday through Saturday, 11 AM to 5 PM; call first
LOCATION: In the United California Bank Building at Wilshire and Camden.

This gallery specializes in traditional tribal art from Africa and Oceania, but sometimes offers objects from antiquity. Established in 1955 by Harry Franklin, it is now owned and directed by his daughter, Valerie. The gallery also has a selection of scholarly publications that relate to the fields represented.

GALLERY K

8406 Melrose Avenue
Los Angeles, California 90069
(213) 651-5282
HOURS: Tuesday through Saturday, noon to 5:30 PM
LOCATION: East of La Cienega, at Melrose Place.

Gallery K deals in primitive art from Oceania, West Africa, and Zaire. The owner of the gallery is Barry Kitkin.

IMAGE OF THE INUIT GALLERY

Contempo Westwood Center
10886 Le Conte Avenue
Los Angeles, California 90024
(213) 473-4152
HOURS: Monday through Friday, 10 AM to 5:30 PM
LOCATION: In Westwood Village on Le Conte Avenue, between Weyburn Avenue and Westwood Boulevard

In the Eskimo language, "inuit" means the people. Image of the Inuit exhibits Eskimo art from Canada and Alaska. The gallery, owned by Janet Tani, offers sculpture, graphics, wallhangings, and basketry, as well as a fine selection of publications on Eskimo art.

THE MANDELL GALLERY

472 North Robertson Boulevard
Los Angeles, California 90048
(213) 652-2396
HOURS: Monday through Friday, 10:30 AM to 5:30 PM;
    Saturday, noon to 4 PM
LOCATION: Near Melrose Avenue.

This gallery, recently opened by Elizabeth Mandell, features West Coast artists who work in clay, fiber, and glass. Objects included in the monthly exhibits are more sculptural than utilitarian.

MANY HORSES GALLERY

740 North La Cienega
Los Angeles, California 90069
(213) 659-0737
HOURS: Tuesday through Saturday, 10 AM to 5 PM
LOCATION: Between La Cienega and Melrose.

This gallery specializes in contemporary fine art of the Southwest. Established in 1973 by Roy LoBianco and Merle Drake, the Many Horses Gallery features paintings, drawings, bronzes, lithographs, and ceramics by Indian artists or artists who use western themes. Ceramics are generally bought directly from artists working on Indian reservations. Exhibits change four to six times each year.

SERISAWA GALLERY

8320 Melrose Avenue (Suite 103)
Los Angeles, California 90069
(213) 651-3526
HOURS: Tuesday through Saturday, 12:30 to 5 PM
LOCATION: Just east of La Cienega Boulevard.

This small gallery specializes in antique Japanese Ukiyo-e prints from the Edo period. These are woodblock prints, both monochrome and colored, made from the mid-seventeenth through the mid-eighteenth centuries. They generally feature pictures of the ''floating world,'' including theatre stars, courtesans, and caricatures.

STENDAHL ART GALLERY

7055-65 Hillside Avenue
Hollywood, California 90068
(213) 876-7740
HOURS: Monday through Saturday, 10 AM to 5 PM, by
    appointment
LOCATION: Hillside is parallel to Franklin Boulevard, between La Brea and Outpost. The nearest cross-street is El Cerritos.

Alfred Stendahl is a highly respected dealer who sells ancient, primitive, and pre-Columbian art. The gallery is adjacent to his Hollywood Hills home.

DAVID STUART GALLERIES

748½ La Cienega Boulevard
Los Angeles, California 90069
(213) 652-7422
HOURS: Tuesday through Saturday, 1 to 5 PM
LOCATION: Between Melrose and Santa Monica.

The David Stuart Galleries specialize in pre-Columbian and African art. Occasionally, American Indian art will be shown. The gallery space is shared with the Jacqueline Anhalt Gallery, which features contemporary work by Southern California artists.

THE SUMMA GALLERIES

342 North Rodeo Drive
Beverly Hills, California 90210
(213) 278-4434
HOURS: Monday through Friday, 9 AM to 5 PM
LOCATION: On Rodeo Drive, between Wilshire and
Santa Monica Boulevards.

Serving museums and collectors throughout the country, Summa specializes in Roman, Greek, and Etruscan art. It offers ancient jewelry and sculpture, with an emphasis on pottery. The gallery is directed by Dr. Jane Cody.

LARRY WHITELEY GALLERIES OF AMERICAN FOLK ART

303 North Sweetzer Avenue
Los Angeles, California 90048
(213) 658-8820
HOURS: Open seven days a week by appointment only.
The first week of an exhibit usually has regular gallery hours.
LOCATION: Between Third Street and Melrose Avenue.

This unique gallery, established in 1978, specializes in nineteenth- and twentieth-century American folk art. It features quilts, hooked rugs, naive painting and sculpture, scrimshaw, weathervanes, whirligigs, and other objects that fall into the somewhat undefined category of folk art. Early scientific instruments and antique photographs are also available. Exhibits, which change every three months, generally have a specific theme (animals, hearts, marine paintings) or present a particular form of folk art (weathervanes, canes, tramp art). Although the gallery is geared to serious collectors, it welcomes novices, who should not be discouraged by the appointment-only policy.

PHOTOGRAPHY GALLERIES

The debate as to whether or not photography is art has more or less been put to rest. A number of contemporary artists use photography or photographic processes as part of their work, and several contemporary galleries, including Rosamund Felsen and Janus, exhibit photographs on a regular basis. Only galleries that sell nothing but photography are included in this section.

The following non-commercial institutions also emphasize photography: ARCO Center for Visual Art, Brooks Institute Photographic Gallery, California Museum of Photography (UC Riverside), Cameravision, Los Angeles Center for Photographic Studies, Mount St. Mary's College Fine Art Gallery, and the Orange Coast College Photography Gallery.

B.C. SPACE

235 Forest Avenue
Laguna Beach, California 92615
(714) 497-1880
HOURS: Tuesday through Saturday, 11:30 AM to 5:30 PM
LOCATION: Just off Pacific Coast Highway, on the south
side of the street. The gallery is upstairs.

B.C. Space evolved from a photographic laboratory service. Its two owners, Jerry Burchfield and Mark Chamberlain, built a gallery as part of their laboratory and started to exhibit the work of local artists. Now, in addition to providing photographic art services, they also offer workshops and classes in their studio space. The gallery gives young, unknown photographers an opportunity to exhibit their work, and is beginning to branch out to feature more established artists.

CITYSCAPE FOTO GALLERY

97 East Colorado Boulevard
Pasadena, California 91109
(213) 796-2036
HOURS: Tuesday, Thursday, and Saturday, noon to 5 PM;
   Wednesday, 7 to 9 PM
LOCATION: West of Arroyo Seco Parkway and East of
   the Norton Simon Museum of Art.

Cityscape primarily exhibits contemporary photography. Owner Lorenzo Hernandez, an industrial engineer whose work schedule accounts for the somewhat erratic gallery hours, says much of the work he displays is documentary in nature and not always marketable. Cityscape has presented the work of master contemporary Mexican photographer M. Alvarez Bravo and represents younger artists such as Morrie Camhi, Michael P. Smith, and Arthur Takayama. The gallery also has a small selection of vintage photographs.

G. RAY HAWKINS

7224 Melrose Avenue
Los Angeles, California 90036
(213) 550-1504
HOURS: Tuesday, 11 AM to 9 PM; Wednesday through
   Saturday, 11 AM to 5 PM
LOCATION: Two blocks west of La Brea.

Specializing in rare, vintage, and contemporary photographs, G. Ray Hawkins is considered the premiere photography gallery in the area. Ten exhibits each year feature major contemporary photographers as well as twentieth-century masters such as Ansel Adams, Henri Cartier-Bresson, Paul Outerbridge, Richard Avedon, Robert Frank, W. Eugene Smith, Philippe Halsman, Edward Weston, and George Hurrell.

Exhibits often integrate vintage and contemporary works to explore issues such as content, process, and formal issues within the medium. Contemporary photographers represented by the gallery include Garry Winogrand, Jo Anne Callis, Richard Misrach, Eileen Cowin, Jerry Burchfield, Judy Dater, Alica Steinhardt, Harry Bowers, and Anthony Friedkin.

The gallery, which was established in 1975, offers an extensive selection of fine-art photography books, posters, and portfolios. It also publishes a monthly *PhotoBulletin* which presents interviews and articles by and with major photographers.

LIGHT

800 North LaCienega
Los Angeles, California 90069
(213) 652-2681
HOURS: Tuesday through Sunday, 11 AM to 6 PM
LOCATION: Between Melrose Avenue and Santa Monica
   Boulevard

Light, a major New York photography gallery, recently opened this space in Los Angeles. It has photographs by twentieth-century masters such as Ansel Adams, Fred Sommers, Minor White, and Walker Evans as well as the work of contemporary photographers, primarily from the East Coast. The gallery, directed by Renato Danese, will present New York artists not represented by Light but who do not have exhibition outlets on the West Coast. Light also plans to introduce West Coast photographers in its New York gallery.

SUSAN SPIRITUS GALLERY

3336 Via Lido
Newport Beach, California 92663
(714) 673-5110
HOURS: Tuesday through Saturday, 11 AM, to 5 PM
LOCATION: Near Newport Boulevard.

Exclusively devoted to contemporary photography, the Susan Spiritus Gallery primarily represents emerging photographers from Europe and the United States. Some of the better-known photographers include Paul Caponigro, George Tice, Robert Heinecken, Jo Ann Callis, and John DiVola. The two-story gallery has two exhibition spaces: a portfolio or group show of the forty to forty-five artists represented by the gallery is on the first floor, while the work of one or two photographers is featured in changing exhibits upstairs. In the summer, the "8 x 10" show features eight works by ten new photographers.

STEPHEN WHITE'S GALLERY OF PHOTOGRAPHY

835 North La Cienega Boulevard
Los Angeles, California 90069
(213) 657-6995
HOURS: Tuesday through Saturday, 11 AM to 5 PM
LOCATION: Between Melrose and Santa Monica.

This gallery, established in 1975, offers a wide selection of photographs by nineteenth- and twentieth-century masters such as Irving Penn, Henri Cartier-Bresson, Harry Calahan, Richard Avedon, and Edward Weston. It also represents several contemporary photographers, including Bruce Barnbaum, Reed Thomas, Herb Quick, and Ruth Bernhard, as well as several European artists. In addition, the gallery presents special one-artist shows, such as a series of rodeo photographs by acclaimed fashion photographer Albert Watson. Exhibits change every five weeks.

BOOKSTORES AND AUCTION HOUSES

The following commercial enterprises cannot be categorized as galleries, but serve the art community.

BOOKSTORES

ART CATALOGUES

8227 Santa Monica Boulevard
Second Floor
Los Angeles, California 90046
(213) 656-8788
HOURS: Tuesday through Saturday, 10 AM to 5:30 PM
LOCATION: Near Crescent Heights, located in a complex
     with several galleries.

Art Catalogues is a unique store that specializes in publications from European and American museums and galleries. It sells catalogues from current exhibitions and also has a large inventory of publications from past shows. The store, which was established by Dagny Janss Corcoran in 1977, concentrates on painting, sculpture, and graphics from 1850. Although it does not sell catalogues on photography or architecture, or general art books, some out-of-print books are available. Catalogues are bought directly from an institution at the time an exhibition opens, and are sold for slightly more than the initial purchase price. Art Catalogues does most of its business by mail, but visitors are welcome to browse in the store's comfortable reading room.

ARTWORKS

66 Windward Avenue
Venice, California 90291
(213) 392-4203
HOURS: Monday through Saturday, 11 AM to 5 PM
LOCATION: North of Venice Boulevard, west of Pacific
     Avenue, just one-half block from the beach

Artworks is a cross between a bookstore and a gallery. It features a large selection of artists' books (books made by artists), art periodicals, postcards made by artists, posters, and a large selection of rubber stamps. Many artists create one-of-a-kind books as well as limited-edition publications. Performances, readings, and exhibitions are also offered at Artworks.

DAVIS AND SCHORR ART BOOKS

1547 Westwood Boulevard
Los Angeles, California 90024
(213) 477-6636
HOURS: Tuesday through Friday, 11 AM to 5 PM; Saturday, 11 AM to 4 PM
LOCATION: Near Ohio Avenue, just north of Santa Monica Boulevard.

This bookstore specializes in rare, out-of-print, and scholarly publications in all fields of fine and applied arts. It also features a selection of books on natural history, limited-edition books, and a selection of original prints and drawings.

Operated by Cal Davis and Elissa Schorr, the store is directed primarily at collectors and artists. It issues lists of its stock and does a large percentage of its business via mail orders.

DAWSON'S BOOK SHOP

535 North Larchmont Boulevard
Los Angeles, California 90004
(213) 469-2186
HOURS: Monday through Saturday, 9 AM to 5:30 PM
LOCATION: Between Melrose and Beverly.

This well-established store (in business since 1905) sells rare, hard-to-find books and specializes in Oriental art books, miniature books (those under three inches), and books concerned with the history of fine printing and graphic arts. It sells primarily to libraries and collectors, but also has a large section of general books.

Dawson's occasionally mounts a special exhibit of fine prints or Japanese prints. The atmosphere in Dawson's is very special and the store is well worth a visit.

HENNESSEY & INGALLS, INC.

Westland Shopping Center
10814 West Pico Boulevard
Los Angeles, California 90064
(213) 474-2541
HOURS: Monday through Friday, 10 AM to 6 PM; Saturday, 10 AM to 5 PM
LOCATION: In West Los Angeles, at Pico and Westwood Boulevards.

Specializing in art and architecture books, Hennessey & Ingalls sells rare, imported, and out-of-print books and collectors' editions. It also has a selection of exhibition catalogues, basic art history books, and scholarly publications in both hardcover and paperback.

LAURENCE MCGILVERY BOOKS ON ART

7863 Girard Avenue
La Jolla, California
(714) 454-4443
HOURS: Monday through Saturday, 11 AM to 5 PM; call for appointment
LOCATION: Near Prospect, at the corner of Wall Street.

Laurence McGilvery specializes in fine-art publications and is known for its large inventory of back issues of major art periodicals, including *Art Forum, Art in America,* and *Art International.* It also carries museum catalogues, out-of-print scholarly books, and rare books. The store, which has been in business for over twenty years, does not conduct searches and tends to charge moderate prices.

ZEITLIN AND VER BRUGGE

815 North La Cienega Boulevard
Los Angeles, California 90069
(213) 652-0784 or 655-7581
HOURS: Monday through Friday, 9 AM to 5 PM
LOCATION: Between Melrose and Santa Monica Boulevard.

Zeitlin and ver Brugge, located in the landmark "red barn" on La Cienega, is a combination gallery and bookstore. The bookstore carries rare books, publications on the history of medicine and science, fine-press books, and art books, both new and out of print. This is not your average walk-in-and-browse bookstore, and visitors must ring a bell to be admitted. For information on the gallery, which sells fine prints, please refer to the listing under traditional galleries.

AUCTION HOUSES

CHRISTIE'S

Christie, Manson and Woods International, Inc.
Suite 328
9350 Wilshire Boulevard
Beverly Hills, California 90212
(213) 275-5534

This west-coast branch of the famous London auction house opened in 1978. Christie's specializes in fine and decorative arts but also auctions such things as vintage automobiles and airplanes. It does not have a sales room and, instead, rents space to display objects prior to an auction. Automobiles and airplanes, for instance, were exhibited in the Los Angeles Convention Center. There is no charge to view the objects, and major art auctions are announced in the *Los Angeles Times* Calendar Section. Catalogues which are published for all major shows give an estimated price for what an item might bring at auction.

SOTHEBY PARKE BERNET

7660 Beverly Boulevard
Los Angeles, California
(213) 937-5130

Sotheby's established in London in 1744, is the oldest fine-art auction firm in the world. It offers a variety of things at auction, from antique trains to furniture, jewelry, and masterpiece paintings. Prior to every auction, Sotheby's displays all of the objects to be sold in special exhibition galleries. There is no charge to view the exhibits, which offer an opportunity to see objects that may never again be on public display. A catalogue is prepared for major auctions and may be purchased. As in any auction operation, Sotheby Parke Bernet offers an appraisal service. A few times a year during "Heirloom Days," members of the general public can bring in cherished objects for a free appraisal. The Los Angeles branch of this auction house is one of thirty-three around the world.

INDEX

INSTITUTIONAL INDEX

ART MUSEUMS

HISTORIC HOUSES

CHILDRENS MUSEUMS

GEOGRAPHICAL INDEX

Listings in the geographical index are organized in clusters to indicate which places are in the same general areas. Major geographical divisions include Western Los Angeles County, Central Los Angeles County, Southern Los Angeles County, Orange County, San Diego County, Santa Barbara County, the San Fernando Valley, Ventura, the Inland Empire, and Pasadena, and each of these is divided into smaller areas.